Slow Cooker

101 recipes

Publications International, Ltd.

Pictured on the front cover: Spanish Paella with Chicken and Sausage *(page 74).*

Pictured on the back cover *(left to right):* Slow Cooker Asian Short Ribs *(page 58)* and Chunky Ranch Potatoes *(page 140).*

ISBN-13: 978-1-4508-2164-3
ISBN-10: 1-4508-2164-2

Library of Congress Control Number: 2011921196

Manufactured in China.

8 7 6 5 4 3 2 1

Microwave Cooking: Microwave ovens vary in wattage. Use the cooking times as guidelines and check for doneness before adding more time.

Preparation/Cooking Times: Preparation times are based on the approximate amount of time required to assemble the recipe before cooking, baking, chilling or serving. These times include preparation steps such as measuring, chopping and mixing. The fact that some preparations and cooking can be done simultaneously is taken into account. Preparation of optional ingredients and serving suggestions is not included.

Publications International, Ltd.

table of contents

Tropical Chicken Wings
page 40

Blue Cheese Potatoes
page 127

shrimp fondue dip
makes about 5 cups

    1 pound medium raw shrimp, peeled
    ½ cup water
    ½ teaspoon salt, divided
    2 tablespoons butter, softened
    4 teaspoons Dijon mustard
    6 slices thick-sliced white bread, crusts removed*
    1 cup milk
    2 eggs
    ¼ teaspoon black pepper
    2 cups (8 ounces) shredded Gruyère or Swiss cheese
    French bread, sliced

Thick-sliced bread is often sold as "Texas toast" in supermarket bread aisles.

slow cooker directions

1. Coat slow cooker with nonstick cooking spray. Place shrimp, water and ¼ teaspoon salt in small saucepan. Cover; cook over medium heat 3 minutes or until shrimp are pink and opaque. Drain shrimp, reserving ½ cup cooking liquid.

2. Combine butter and mustard in small bowl. Spread mixture onto white bread slices. Cut bread into 1-inch cubes.

3. Whisk milk, eggs, reserved cooking liquid, remaining ¼ teaspoon salt and pepper in small bowl.

4. Spread one third of bread cubes in bottom of slow cooker. Top with one third of shrimp. Sprinkle with one third of Gruyère cheese. Repeat layers. Pour in egg mixture. Press down on bread mixture to absorb liquid. Line lid with 2 paper towels.

5. Cover; cook on LOW 2 hours or until heated through and thickened. Serve with French bread.

prep time: 15 minutes • **cook time:** 2 hours

firecracker black bean dip
makes 8 to 10 servings

    1 can (16 ounces) refried black beans
  ¾ cup salsa
    1 poblano pepper, seeded and minced
    1 teaspoon chili powder
  ½ cup crumbled queso fresco*
    3 green onions, sliced
      Tortilla chips

**Queso fresco is a mild white Mexican cheese. If unavailable,
you may substitute shredded Monterey Jack or Cheddar cheese.*

slow cooker directions

1. Combine beans, salsa, poblano pepper and chili powder in slow cooker. Cover; cook on LOW 4 hours or on HIGH 2 hours.

2. Sprinkle with queso fresco and green onions. Serve warm with tortilla chips.

prep time: 5 minutes • **cook time:** 4 hours (LOW) or 2 hours (HIGH)

swiss cheese fondue

makes 6 servings

 1 clove garlic, cut in half
 1 can (10½ ounces) CAMPBELL'S®
     Condensed Chicken Broth
 2 cans (10¾ ounces each) CAMPBELL'S®
     Condensed Cheddar Cheese Soup
 1 cup water
 ½ cup Chablis or other dry white wine
 1 tablespoon Dijon-style mustard
 1 tablespoon cornstarch
 4 cups shredded Emmentaler or Gruyère cheese
     (about 1 pound), at room temperature
 ¼ teaspoon ground nutmeg
    Dash ground black pepper
    PEPPERIDGE FARM® Garlic Bread, prepared and
       cut into cubes
    Fresh vegetables

slow cooker directions

1. Rub the inside of a 5½-quart slow cooker with the cut sides of the garlic. Discard the garlic. Stir the broth, soup, water, wine, mustard, cornstarch, cheese, nutmeg and black pepper in the cooker.

2. Cover and cook on LOW for 1 hour or until the cheese is melted, stirring occasionally.

3. Serve with the bread and vegetables on skewers for dipping.

kitchen tip: This recipe may be doubled.

prep time: 10 minutes • **cook time:** 1 hour

bagna cauda
makes 10 to 12 servings

¾ **cup olive oil**
6 **tablespoons (¾ stick) butter, softened**
12 **anchovy fillets, drained**
6 **cloves garlic, peeled**
⅛ **teaspoon red pepper flakes**
Assorted foods for dipping: endive spears, cauliflower florets, cucumber spears, carrot sticks, zucchini spears, red bell pepper strips, sugar snap peas or Italian bread slices

slow cooker directions

1. Combine oil, butter, anchovies, garlic and red pepper flakes in food processor; process until smooth. Transfer to slow cooker.

2. Cover; cook on LOW 2 hours or until heated through. Serve with assorted dippers.

note: Bagna cauda is a warm Italian dip similar to fondue. The name is derived from "bagno caldo," meaning "warm bath" in Italian. This dip should be kept warm while serving.

prep time: 10 minutes • **cook time:** 2 hours

creamy artichoke-parmesan dip

makes 4 cups

> 2 cans (about 14 ounces each) artichoke hearts, drained and chopped
> 2 cups (8 ounces) shredded mozzarella cheese
> 1½ cups grated Parmesan cheese
> 1½ cups mayonnaise
> ½ cup finely chopped onion
> ½ teaspoon dried oregano
> ¼ teaspoon garlic powder
> 4 pita bread rounds
> Assorted cut-up vegetables

slow cooker directions

1. Combine artichokes, mozzarella cheese, Parmesan cheese, mayonnaise, onion, oregano and garlic powder in slow cooker; mix well.

2. Cover; cook on LOW 2 hours.

3. Just before serving, cut pita into wedges. Serve dip with pita wedges and vegetables.

hearty calico bean dip
makes 12 servings

¾ **pound ground beef**
1 **can (about 16 ounces) baked beans**
1 **can (about 15 ounces) Great Northern beans, rinsed and drained**
1 **can (about 15 ounces) kidney beans, rinsed and drained**
½ **pound sliced bacon, crisp-cooked and crumbled**
1 **onion, chopped**
½ **cup packed brown sugar**
½ **cup ketchup**
1 **tablespoon cider vinegar**
1 **teaspoon yellow mustard**
  Tortilla chips

slow cooker directions

1. Brown beef in large skillet over medium-high heat 6 to 8 minutes, stirring to break up meat. Drain fat. Transfer beef to slow cooker.

2. Add baked beans, Great Northern beans, kidney beans, bacon, onion, brown sugar, ketchup, vinegar and mustard to slow cooker; mix well.

3. Cover; cook on LOW 4 hours or on HIGH 2 hours. Serve with tortilla chips.

apricot and brie dip
makes 8 to 12 servings

½ cup dried apricots, finely chopped
⅓ cup plus 1 tablespoon apricot preserves,
    divided
¼ cup apple juice
1 (2-pound) brie, rind removed, cut into
    cubes
Crackers

slow cooker directions

1. Combine dried apricots, ⅓ cup apricot preserves and apple juice in slow cooker. Cover; cook on HIGH 40 minutes.

2. Stir in brie. Cover; cook 30 minutes or until melted. Stir in remaining 1 tablespoon preserves. Serve with crackers.

prep time: 10 minutes • **cook time:** 1 hour 10 minutes

tip: Dried apricots have been pitted, but not peeled, before drying. They are treated with sulfur dioxide to preserve their color.

italiano fondue
makes 2 cups

1¾ cups PREGO® Traditional or Tomato, Basil & Garlic Italian Sauce
¼ cup dry red wine
1 cup shredded mozzarella cheese (about 4 ounces)
Assorted Dippers: Warm PEPPERIDGE FARM® Garlic Bread, cut into cubes; meatballs; sliced cooked Italian pork sausage; breaded mozzarella sticks; sliced red pepper and/or whole mushrooms

slow cooker directions

1. Heat the Italian Sauce and wine in a 3-quart saucepan over medium heat for 5 minutes.

2. Pour the sauce mixture into a slow cooker set on LOW. Sprinkle with the cheese. Let stand for 5 minutes or until the cheese is melted. Serve the fondue warm with the Assorted Dippers.

prep time: 5 minutes • **cook time:** 10 minutes

pepperoni pizza dip with breadstick dippers
makes 8 servings

    1 jar (about 14 ounces) pizza sauce
  ¾ cup chopped turkey pepperoni
    4 green onions, chopped
    1 can (2¼ ounces) sliced black olives, drained
  ½ teaspoon dried oregano
    1 cup (4 ounces) shredded mozzarella cheese
    1 package (3 ounces) cream cheese, softened
      Breadsticks

slow cooker directions

1. Combine pizza sauce, pepperoni, green onions, olives and oregano in slow cooker.

2. Cover; cook on LOW 2 hours or until heated through.

3. Stir in mozzarella cheese and cream cheese until melted and well blended. Serve with breadsticks.

prep time: 10 minutes • **cook time:** 2 hours

chunky pinto bean dip
makes about 5 cups dip

   2 cans (about 15 ounces each) pinto beans,
      rinsed and drained
   1 can (about 14 ounces) diced tomatoes
      with green chiles
   1 cup chopped onion
 ⅔ cup chunky salsa
   1 tablespoon vegetable oil
1½ teaspoons minced garlic
   1 teaspoon ground coriander
   1 teaspoon ground cumin
1½ cups (6 ounces) shredded Mexican cheese blend or
      Cheddar cheese
 ¼ cup chopped fresh cilantro
      Blue corn or other tortilla chips

slow cooker directions

1. Combine beans, tomatoes, onion, salsa, oil, garlic, coriander and cumin in slow cooker; mix well.

2. Cover; cook on LOW 5 to 6 hours.

3. Partially mash bean mixture with potato masher. Stir in cheese blend and cilantro. Serve with tortilla chips.

prep time: 12 minutes • **cook time:** 5 to 6 hours

slow cooker cheese dip
makes 16 to 18 servings

1 pound ground beef
1 pound bulk Italian sausage
1 package (16 ounces) pasteurized process cheese product, cubed
1 can (11 ounces) sliced jalapeño peppers, drained
1 onion, diced
2 cups (8 ounces) Cheddar cheese, cubed
1 package (8 ounces) cream cheese, cubed
1 container (8 ounces) cottage cheese
1 container (8 ounces) sour cream
1 can (8 ounces) diced tomatoes, drained
3 cloves garlic, minced
Salt and black pepper
Tortilla chips

slow cooker directions

1. Brown ground beef and sausage in large skillet over medium-high heat 6 to 8 minutes, stirring to break up meat. Drain fat. Transfer to slow cooker.

2. Add process cheese, jalapeño peppers, onion, Cheddar cheese, cream cheese, cottage cheese, sour cream, tomatoes and garlic to slow cooker. Season with salt and black pepper.

3. Cover; cook on HIGH 1½ to 2 hours or until cheeses are melted. Serve with tortilla chips.

bean dip for a crowd
makes 6 cups

- 1½ cups dried black beans
- 1½ cups dried pinto beans
- 3 tablespoons chopped fresh Italian parsley
- 2 tablespoons minced onion
- 1 package (about 1 ounce) hot taco seasoning mix
- 3 chicken bouillon cubes
- 2 bay leaves
- 1 jar (16 ounces) chunky salsa
- 2 tablespoons lime juice
  Tortilla chips

slow cooker directions

1. Place beans in large bowl; cover with water. Soak 6 hours or overnight. (To quick-soak beans, place beans in large saucepan; cover with water. Bring to a boil over high heat. Boil 2 minutes. Remove from heat; let soak, covered, 1 hour.) Drain beans; discard water.

2. Combine beans, 5 cups water, parsley, onion, seasoning mix, bouillon cubes and bay leaves in slow cooker.

3. Cover; cook on LOW 9 to 10 hours. Add additional water, ½ cup at a time, if needed. Remove and discard bay leaves.

4. Place half of bean mixture in food processor. Add salsa and lime juice; process until smooth. Return to slow cooker; stir to combine. Serve with tortilla chips.

artichoke and nacho cheese dip

makes about 1 quart

> **2 cans (10¾ ounces each) condensed nacho cheese soup, undiluted**
> **1 can (about 14 ounces) quartered artichoke hearts, drained and coarsely chopped**
> **1 cup (4 ounces) shredded pepper jack cheese**
> **1 can (4 ounces) evaporated milk**
> **2 tablespoons minced fresh chives, divided**
> **½ teaspoon paprika**
> **Crackers**

slow cooker directions

1. Combine soup, artichokes, pepper jack cheese, evaporated milk, 1 tablespoon chives and paprika in slow cooker. Cover; cook on LOW 2 hours.

2. Stir well; sprinkle with remaining 1 tablespoon chives. Serve with crackers.

prep time: 5 minutes • **cook time:** 2 hours

chili con queso
makes 3 cups

- 1 package (16 ounces) pasteurized process cheese product, cubed
- 1 can (10 ounces) diced tomatoes with green chiles
- 1 cup sliced green onions
- 2 teaspoons ground coriander
- 2 teaspoons ground cumin
- ¾ teaspoon hot pepper sauce
  Green onion strips (optional)
  Jalapeño pepper slices (optional)*
  Tortilla chips

Jalapeño peppers can sting and irritate the skin, so wear rubber gloves when handling peppers and do not touch your eyes.

slow cooker directions

1. Combine process cheese, tomatoes, green onions, coriander, cumin and hot pepper sauce in slow cooker; stir until well blended.

2. Cover; cook on LOW 2 hours or until heated through.

3. Garnish with green onion strips and jalapeño pepper slices. Serve with tortilla chips.

serving suggestion: Chili con Queso can also be served with pita bread chips. To prepare, cut pita bread rounds into triangles. Arrange them in a single layer on a baking sheet and toast in a preheated 400°F oven 5 minutes or until crisp.

creamy cheesy spinach dip

makes about 4 cups

2 packages (10 ounces each) frozen chopped spinach, thawed
2 cups chopped onions
1 teaspoon salt
½ teaspoon garlic powder
¼ teaspoon black pepper
12 ounces pepper jack-flavored pasteurized process cheese product, cubed
Assorted crackers

slow cooker directions

1. Drain spinach and squeeze dry, reserving ¾ cup liquid. Combine spinach, reserved liquid, onions, salt, garlic powder and black pepper in slow cooker; mix well.

2. Cover; cook on HIGH 1 ½ hours.

3. Stir in process cheese; cook 30 minutes or until melted. Serve with crackers.

tip: To thaw spinach quickly, remove paper wrapper from spinach containers; place on microwavable plate. Microwave on HIGH 3 to 4 minutes or just until thawed.

con & cheese dip

makes 32 servings

- 2 packages (8 ounces each) cream cheese, softened and cut into cubes
- 4 cups (16 ounces) shredded sharp Cheddar cheese
- 1 cup evaporated milk
- 2 tablespoons yellow mustard
- 1 tablespoon chopped onion
- 2 teaspoons Worcestershire sauce
- ½ teaspoon salt
- ¼ teaspoon hot pepper sauce (optional)
- 1 pound bacon, crisp-cooked and crumbled
  Assorted cut-up vegetables or French bread slices

slow cooker directions

1. Combine cream cheese, Cheddar cheese, evaporated milk, mustard, onion, Worcestershire sauce, salt and hot pepper sauce, if desired, in slow cooker.

2. Cover; cook on LOW 1 hour or until cheese is melted, stirring occasionally. Stir in bacon. Serve with vegetables or bread slices.

prep time: 5 minutes • **cook time:** 1 hour

easy taco dip
makes about 3 cups

- ½ **pound ground beef**
- 1 **cup frozen corn**
- ½ **cup chopped onion**
- ½ **cup salsa**
- ½ **cup mild taco sauce**
- 1 **can (4 ounces) diced mild green chiles, drained**
- 1 **can (4 ounces) sliced black olives, drained**
- 1 **cup (4 ounces) shredded Mexican cheese blend**
- **Sour cream (optional)**
- **Tortilla chips**

slow cooker directions

1. Brown beef in medium skillet over medium-high heat 6 to 8 minutes, stirring to break up meat. Drain fat. Transfer beef to slow cooker.

2. Add corn, onion, salsa, taco sauce, chiles and olives to slow cooker; mix well. Cover; cook on LOW 2 to 3 hours.

3. Just before serving, stir in cheese blend. Top with sour cream, if desired. Serve with tortilla chips.

note: To keep this dip hot through an entire party, simply leave it in the slow cooker set on LOW or WARM.

prep time: 15 minutes • **cook time:** 2 to 3 hours

pizza fondue
makes 20 to 25 servings

½ **pound bulk Italian sausage**
1 **cup chopped onion**
2 **jars (26 ounces each) meatless pasta sauce**
4 **ounces thinly sliced ham, finely chopped**
1 **package (3 ounces) sliced pepperoni, finely chopped**
¼ **teaspoon red pepper flakes**
1 **pound mozzarella cheese, cut into ¾-inch cubes**
1 **loaf Italian or French bread, cut into 1-inch cubes**

slow cooker directions

1. Brown sausage and onion in medium skillet over medium-high heat 6 to 8 minutes, stirring to break up meat. Drain fat. Transfer sausage mixture to slow cooker.

2. Stir in pasta sauce, ham, pepperoni and red pepper flakes. Cover; cook on LOW 3 to 4 hours.

3. Serve with mozzarella cheese and bread cubes.

prep time: 15 minutes • **cook time:** 3 to 4 hours

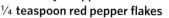

stewed fig and blue cheese dip

makes 6 to 8 servings

    1 tablespoon olive oil
    1 onion, chopped
  ½ cup port wine
    1 package (6 ounces) dried Calimyrna figs,
        finely chopped
  ½ cup orange juice
  ½ cup crumbled blue cheese, divided
    1 tablespoon unsalted butter
      Assorted crackers

slow cooker directions

1. Heat oil in small nonstick skillet over medium-high heat. Add onion; cook 7 minutes or until golden, stirring occasionally. Stir in port and bring to a boil; cook 1 minute.

2. Transfer to slow cooker; stir in figs and orange juice.

3. Cover; cook on HIGH 1 to 1½ hours or until figs are plump and tender. Stir in ¼ cup blue cheese and butter. Sprinkle with remaining ¼ cup blue cheese. Serve with assorted crackers.

prep time: 15 minutes • **cook time:** 1 to 1½ hours

reuben dip
makes 12 servings

  1 jar or bag (about 32 ounces) sauerkraut,
    rinsed and drained
  2 cups (8 ounces) shredded Swiss cheese
  3 packages (2½ ounces each) corned beef,
    shredded
  ½ cup (1 stick) butter, melted
  1 egg, beaten
    Rye cocktail bread

slow cooker directions

1. Combine sauerkraut, Swiss cheese, corned beef, butter and egg in slow cooker. Cover; cook on HIGH 2 hours.

2. Serve with cocktail bread.

> tip: This dip combines all the classic flavors of the famous deli sandwich into a hearty, satisfying treat that is perfect for warming up guests as they come in from the cold during the winter season. A perfect combination of tangy sauerkraut, creamy Swiss cheese and savory corned beef, Reuben Dip has all of your cravings covered.

savory sausage dip
makes 20 servings

1 pound bulk pork sausage
1 package (16 ounces) pasteurized process cheese product, cubed
1 package (16 ounces) Mexican-flavored pasteurized process cheese product, cubed
1 can (16 ounces) refried beans
1 can (10³/₄ ounces) condensed cream of mushroom soup, undiluted
1 onion, chopped
   Tortilla chips

slow cooker directions

1. Brown sausage in large skillet over medium-high heat 6 to 8 minutes, stirring to break up meat. Drain fat. Transfer sausage to slow cooker.

2. Add process cheeses, beans, soup and onion to slow cooker. Stir to combine.

3. Cover; cook on LOW 2 hours or until heated through. Serve with tortilla chips.

chorizo and queso fundido

makes 8 to 12 servings

2 cured chorizo sausages (about 3½ ounces), finely chopped
1 package (8 ounces) cream cheese, cubed
8 ounces Monterey Jack cheese, cubed
8 ounces pasteurized process cheese product, cubed
8 ounces Cheddar cheese, cubed
1 tablespoon Worcestershire sauce
Tortilla chips

slow cooker directions

1. Combine chorizo, cream cheese, Monterey Jack cheese, process cheese, Cheddar cheese and Worcestershire sauce in slow cooker.

2. Cover; cook on HIGH 1 to 1½ hours or until cheese looks very soft. Whisk to blend.

3. *Turn slow cooker to LOW or WARM.* Serve with tortilla chips.

note: In Spanish, queso fundido means "melted cheese," which precisely describes this dish. For a more authentic taste, replace some of the cheeses in this recipe with traditional Mexican cheeses such as queso fresco, chihuahua or cotija.

prep time: 10 minutes • **cook time:** 1 to 1½ hours

warm moroccan-style bean dip
makes 4 to 6 servings

- 2 teaspoons canola oil
- 1 onion, chopped
- 2 cloves garlic, minced
- 2 cans (about 15 ounces each) cannellini beans, rinsed and drained
- ¾ cup drained canned diced tomatoes
- ½ teaspoon ground turmeric (optional)
- ¼ teaspoon *each* salt, ground cumin, ground cinnamon, paprika and black pepper
- ⅛ teaspoon *each* ground cloves and ground red pepper
- 2 tablespoons plain yogurt
- 1 tablespoon water
- ¼ teaspoon dried mint (optional)
  Warm pita bread, cut into wedges

slow cooker directions

1. Heat oil in small skillet over medium-high heat. Add onion; cook and stir 5 minutes or until translucent. Add garlic; cook and stir 30 seconds. Transfer to slow cooker. Stir in beans, tomatoes, turmeric, if desired, salt, cumin, cinnamon, paprika, black pepper, cloves and ground red pepper. Cover; cook on LOW 6 hours.

2. Transfer to food processor or blender; process using on/off pulsing action until coarsely chopped. (Or use immersion blender.) Transfer to bowl.

3. Whisk yogurt and water in small bowl; drizzle over bean dip. Garnish with dried mint. Serve with pita bread wedges.

note: Moroccan cuisine is notable for a wide array of dishes. The cuisine makes use of a wide variety of spices that reflect the many ethnicities that have influenced the country over the centuries. This spice-filled dip is sure to stimulate taste buds and conversation with its combination of exotic flavors.

raspberry-balsamic glazed meatballs
makes about 32 meatballs

- **1 bag (32 ounces) frozen fully cooked meatballs**
- **1 cup raspberry preserves**
- **3 tablespoons sugar**
- **3 tablespoons balsamic vinegar**
- **1 tablespoon plus 1½ teaspoons Worcestershire sauce**
- **¼ teaspoon red pepper flakes**
- **1 tablespoon grated fresh ginger (optional)**

slow cooker directions

1. Coat slow cooker with nonstick cooking spray. Add meatballs.

2. Combine preserves, sugar, vinegar, Worcestershire sauce and red pepper flakes in small microwavable bowl. Microwave on HIGH 45 seconds; stir. Microwave 15 seconds or until melted (mixture will be chunky). Reserve ½ cup preserves mixture. Pour remaining mixture over meatballs; toss to coat. Cover; cook on LOW 5 hours or on HIGH 2½ hours.

3. *Turn slow cooker to HIGH.* Stir in ginger, if desired, and reserved ½ cup preserves mixture. Cook, uncovered, 15 to 20 minutes or until thickened slightly, stirring occasionally.

mini carnitas tacos
makes 12 servings

- 1½ pounds boneless pork loin, cut into 1-inch cubes
- 1 onion, finely chopped
- ½ cup chicken broth
- 1 tablespoon chili powder
- 2 teaspoons ground cumin
- 1 teaspoon dried oregano
- ½ teaspoon minced canned chipotle peppers in adobo sauce (optional)
- ½ cup pico de gallo
- 2 tablespoons chopped fresh cilantro
- ½ teaspoon salt
- 12 (6-inch) corn tortillas
- ¾ cup (3 ounces) shredded sharp Cheddar cheese
- 3 tablespoons sour cream

slow cooker directions

1. Combine pork, onion, broth, chili powder, cumin, oregano and chipotle, if desired, in slow cooker.

2. Cover; cook on LOW 6 hours or on HIGH 3 hours. Pour off excess cooking liquid.

3. Shred pork with two forks. Stir in pico de gallo, cilantro and salt. Cover and keep warm.

4. Cut 3 circles from each tortilla with 2-inch biscuit cutter. Top with pork, Cheddar cheese and sour cream.

note: Carnitas means "little meats" in Spanish. This dish is usually made with an inexpensive cut of pork that is simmered for a long time until it falls to pieces. The meat is then browned in pork fat. The slow cooker makes the long, slow cooking process easy to manage and skipping the final browning lowers the fat content.

prep time: 5 minutes • **cook time:** 6 hours (LOW) or 3 hours (HIGH)

caponata
makes about 5¼ cups

**1 medium eggplant (about 1 pound),
    peeled and cut into ½-inch pieces**

**1 can (about 14 ounces) diced Italian plum
    tomatoes**

1 onion, chopped

1 red bell pepper, cut into ½-inch pieces

½ cup salsa

¼ cup olive oil

2 tablespoons capers, drained

2 tablespoons balsamic vinegar

3 cloves garlic, minced

1 teaspoon dried oregano

¼ teaspoon salt

**⅓ cup packed fresh basil, cut into thin strips
    Toasted Italian or French bread slices**

slow cooker directions

1. Combine eggplant, tomatoes, onion, bell pepper, salsa, oil, capers, vinegar, garlic, oregano and salt in slow cooker. Cover; cook on LOW 7 to 8 hours.

2. Stir in basil. Serve at room temperature with bread slices.

prep time: 20 to 25 minutes • **cook time:** 7 to 8 hours

chicken & vegetable bruschetta

makes 7 servings

1 can (10¾ ounces) CAMPBELL'S®
  Condensed Cream of Mushroom Soup
  (Regular or 98% Fat Free)
1 can (about 14½ ounces) diced tomatoes,
  drained
1 small eggplant, peeled and diced
  (about 2 cups)
1 large zucchini, diced (about 2 cups)
1 small onion, chopped (about ¼ cup)
1 pound skinless, boneless chicken breast halves
¼ cup shredded Parmesan cheese
2 tablespoons chopped fresh parsley or basil leaves
  Thinly sliced Italian bread, toasted

slow cooker directions

1. Stir the soup, tomatoes, eggplant, zucchini and onion in a 6-quart slow cooker. Add the chicken and turn to coat.

2. Cover and cook on LOW for 6 to 7 hours* or until the chicken is fork-tender.

3. Remove the chicken from the cooker to a cutting board and let stand for 5 minutes. Using two forks, shred the chicken. Return the chicken to the cooker. Stir in the cheese and parsley.

4. Serve on the bread slices. Sprinkle with additional Parmesan cheese and chopped parsley, if desired.

Or on HIGH for 4 to 5 hours.

prep time: 15 minutes • **cook time:** 6 to 7 hours

thai chicken wings
makes 8 servings

1 tablespoon peanut oil
5 pounds chicken wings, tips removed and
   split at joints
½ cup coconut milk
1 tablespoon sugar
1 tablespoon Thai green curry paste
1 tablespoon fish sauce
¾ cup prepared spicy peanut sauce

slow cooker directions

1. Heat oil in large nonstick skillet over medium-high heat. Working in batches, cook wings 6 minutes or until browned. Transfer to slow cooker.

2. Stir in coconut milk, sugar, curry paste and fish sauce. Cover; cook on LOW 6 hours or on HIGH 3 hours or until cooked through. Drain cooking liquid and carefully stir in peanut sauce before serving.

prep time: 15 minutes • **cook time:** 6 hours (LOW) or 3 hours (HIGH)

tip: Peanut oil has a faint peanut flavor and a high smoke point. It is a good oil for frying and stir-frying.

asian barbecue skewers
makes 4 to 6 servings

   2 pounds boneless skinless chicken thighs
   ½ cup soy sauce
   ⅓ cup packed brown sugar
   2 tablespoons sesame oil
   3 cloves garlic, minced
   ½ cup thinly sliced green onions (optional)
   1 tablespoon toasted sesame seeds
       (optional)

slow cooker directions

1. Cut each thigh into 4 pieces about 1½ inches thick. Thread chicken onto 7-inch wooden skewers, folding thinner pieces, if necessary. Place skewers in slow cooker, layering as flat as possible.

2. Combine soy sauce, brown sugar, oil and garlic in small bowl. Reserve ⅓ cup sauce. Pour remaining sauce over skewers. Cover; cook on LOW 2 hours. Turn skewers. Cover; cook 1 hour.

3. Transfer skewers to serving platter. Discard cooking liquid. Pour reserved sauce over skewers. Sprinkle with green onions and sesame seeds, if desired.

prep time: 10 minutes • **cook time:** 3 hours

sausage and swiss chard stuffed mushrooms
makes 6 to 8 servings

      2 packages (6 ounces each) cremini mushrooms*
      4 tablespoons olive oil, divided
         Salt and black pepper
    ½ pound bulk pork sausage
    ½ onion, finely chopped
      2 cups chopped Swiss chard
    ¼ teaspoon dried thyme
      2 tablespoons seasoned dry bread crumbs
  1½ cups chicken broth, divided
      2 tablespoons grated Parmesan cheese
      2 tablespoons chopped fresh Italian parsley

Do not substitute white button mushrooms.

slow cooker directions

1. Coat slow cooker with nonstick cooking spray. Wipe mushrooms clean and remove stems. Brush mushrooms inside and out with 3 tablespoons oil. Season with salt and pepper.

2. Heat remaining 1 tablespoon oil in medium skillet over medium heat. Add sausage; cook and stir until browned. Transfer to medium bowl with slotted spoon.

3. Add onion to skillet; cook 3 minutes or until translucent, stirring to scrape up browned bits. Stir in chard and thyme. Cook 1 minute or until chard is wilted. Remove skillet from heat.

4. Add sausage, bread crumbs and 1 tablespoon broth; mix well. Season with salt and pepper. Spoon evenly into mushroom caps.

5. Pour remaining broth into slow cooker. Arrange stuffed mushrooms in bottom. Cover; cook on HIGH 3 hours or until tender. Remove mushrooms with slotted spoon; discard cooking liquid. Combine Parmesan cheese and parsley in small bowl; sprinkle onto mushrooms.

prep time: 20 minutes • **cook time:** 3 hours

slow-cooked pulled pork sliders

makes 12 mini sandwiches

**1 can (10¾ ounces) CAMPBELL'S®
    Condensed Tomato Soup**
½ cup packed brown sugar
¼ cup cider vinegar
1 teaspoon garlic powder
**1 boneless pork shoulder roast
    (3½ to 4½ pounds)**
**2 packages (15 ounces each) PEPPERIDGE FARM®
    Slider Mini Sandwich Rolls**
Hot pepper sauce (optional)

slow cooker directions

1. Stir the soup, brown sugar, vinegar and garlic powder in a 6-quart slow cooker. Add the pork and turn to coat.

2. Cover and cook on LOW for 8 to 9 hours* or until the pork is fork-tender. Spoon off any fat.

3. Remove the pork from the cooker to a cutting board and let stand for 10 minutes. Using two forks, shred the pork. Return the pork to the cooker.

4. Divide the pork mixture among the rolls. Serve with the hot pepper sauce, if desired.

Or on HIGH for 5 to 6 hours.

prep time: 10 minutes • **cook time:** 8 to 9 hours

sweet & sour cocktail franks

makes about 4 dozen cocktail franks

2 packages (8 ounces each) cocktail franks
½ cup ketchup or chili sauce
½ cup apricot preserves
1 teaspoon hot pepper sauce
Additional hot pepper sauce (optional)

slow cooker directions

1. Combine franks, ketchup, preserves and 1 teaspoon hot pepper sauce in slow cooker; mix well. Cover; cook on LOW 2 to 3 hours.

2. Serve warm or at room temperature with additional hot pepper sauce, if desired.

prep time: 5 minutes • **cook time:** 2 to 3 hours

tip: This recipe allows you to customize how spicy you want the finished dish to be. Choose ketchup to keep it on the mild side or opt for chili sauce to up the heat quotient. If chili sauce doesn't increase the fire enough for your taste, you can ratchet up the amount of hot pepper sauce as needed.

tropical chicken wings
makes 6 to 8 servings

    1 jar (12 ounces) pineapple preserves
  ½ cup chopped green onions
  ½ cup soy sauce
    3 tablespoons lime juice
    2 tablespoons pomegranate molasses or honey
    1 tablespoon minced garlic
    2 teaspoons sriracha sauce*
  ¼ teaspoon ground allspice
    3 pounds chicken wings, tips removed and split at joints
    1 tablespoon toasted sesame seeds

Sriracha is a spicy sauce made from dried chiles that is used as a condiment in several Asian cuisines. It can be found in the ethnic section of major supermarkets, but an equal amount of hot pepper sauce may be substituted.

slow cooker directions

1. Combine preserves, green onions, soy sauce, lime juice, pomegranate molasses, garlic, sriracha sauce and allspice in slow cooker; stir well.

2. Add chicken wings; stir to coat. Cover; cook on LOW 3 to 4 hours.

3. Sprinkle with sesame seeds just before serving.

tip: Pomegranate molasses is a syrup made from pomegranate juice cooked with sugar. You can easily make your own if it isn't available in the ethnic foods aisle of your local supermarket. For this recipe, bring ½ cup pomegranate juice, 2 tablespoons sugar and 1 teaspoon lemon juice to a boil in a small saucepan over medium-high heat. Cook and stir until reduced to about 2 tablespoons.

barbecued meatballs
makes about 4 dozen meatballs

   2 pounds ground beef
1⅓ cups ketchup, divided
   1 egg, lightly beaten
   3 tablespoons seasoned dry bread crumbs
   2 tablespoons dried onion flakes
  ¾ teaspoon garlic salt
  ½ teaspoon black pepper
   1 cup packed light brown sugar
   1 can (6 ounces) tomato paste
  ¼ cup reduced-sodium soy sauce
  ¼ cup cider vinegar
1½ teaspoons hot pepper sauce

slow cooker directions

1. Preheat oven to 350°F. Combine ground beef, ⅓ cup ketchup, egg, bread crumbs, onion flakes, garlic salt and black pepper in large bowl. Mix lightly but thoroughly; shape into 1-inch meatballs.

2. Arrange meatballs in single layer on two 15×10-inch jelly-roll pans. Bake 18 minutes or until browned. Transfer meatballs to slow cooker.

3. Mix remaining 1 cup ketchup, brown sugar, tomato paste, soy sauce, vinegar and hot pepper sauce in medium bowl. Pour over meatballs. Cover; cook on LOW 4 hours. Serve with cocktail picks.

barbecued franks: Arrange two (12-ounce) packages or three (8-ounce) packages cocktail franks in slow cooker. Combine 1 cup ketchup, brown sugar, tomato paste, soy sauce, vinegar and hot pepper sauce in medium bowl; pour over franks. Cover; cook on LOW 4 hours.

prep time: 25 minutes • **cook time:** 4 hours

sun-dried tomato appetizer torte

makes 8 servings

3 cups chopped onions

3 jars (about 7 ounces each) oil-packed
   sun-dried tomatoes, drained and finely
   chopped

3 tablespoons sugar

1 tablespoon minced garlic

1 piece (2 inches) fresh ginger, peeled and grated

1 teaspoon herbes de Provence

½ teaspoon salt

½ cup red wine vinegar

1 package (8 ounces) cream cheese
   Fresh basil sprigs (optional)
   Assorted crackers

slow cooker directions

1. Place onions, tomatoes, sugar, garlic, ginger, herbes de Provence and salt in slow cooker. Pour in vinegar; stir gently.

2. Cover; cook on LOW 4 to 5 hours or on HIGH 3 hours, stirring occasionally. Let mixture cool before using.

3. To serve, slice cream cheese in half horizontally. (Use unflavored dental floss for clean cut.) Spread ⅓ cup tomato mixture onto one cream cheese half. Top with second cream cheese half and spread ⅓ cup tomato mixture on top.

4. Garnish with fresh basil sprigs and serve with crackers. Wrap and refrigerate until just before serving. Refrigerate or freeze remaining tomato mixture for another use.

sweet and spicy sausage rounds

makes about 16 servings

1 pound kielbasa sausage, cut into ¼-inch-thick rounds
⅔ cup blackberry jam
⅓ cup steak sauce
1 tablespoon yellow mustard
½ teaspoon ground allspice

slow cooker directions

1. Combine sausage, jam, steak sauce, mustard and allspice in slow cooker; toss to coat completely.

2. Cover; cook on HIGH 3 hours or until sauce is thickened and sausage is glazed.

3. Serve with decorative cocktail picks.

tip: Kielbasa is a traditional pork or beef sausage from Eastern Europe. While there are many different types of sausage that fall into this general category, there is one in particular that we mean when we call for kielbasa in the United States. Garlicky and rich in flavor, this thick smoked sausage is available alongside other sausages and sliced deli meats in the refrigerated case.

mini swiss steak sandwiches
makes 16 to 18 sandwiches

      2 tablespoons all-purpose flour
    1/4 teaspoon salt
    1/4 teaspoon black pepper
  13/4 pounds boneless beef chuck steak, about 1 inch thick
      2 tablespoons vegetable oil
      1 onion, sliced
      1 green bell pepper, sliced
      1 clove garlic, sliced
      1 cup canned stewed tomatoes
    3/4 cup condensed beef consommé, undiluted
      2 teaspoons Worcestershire sauce
      1 bay leaf
      2 tablespoons cornstarch
      2 packages (12 ounces each) sweet Hawaiian dinner rolls

slow cooker directions

1. Coat slow cooker with nonstick cooking spray. Combine flour, salt and black pepper in large resealable food storage bag. Add steak; shake to coat.

2. Heat oil in large skillet over high heat. Add steak and brown on both sides. Transfer to slow cooker.

3. Add onion and bell pepper to skillet; cook and stir over medium heat 3 minutes or until softened. Add garlic; cook and stir 30 seconds. Pour mixture over steak.

4. Add tomatoes, consommé, Worcestershire sauce and bay leaf. Cover; cook on HIGH 3½ hours or until steak is tender. Transfer steak to cutting board. Remove and discard bay leaf.

5. Whisk cornstarch into 2 tablespoons cooking liquid in small bowl until smooth. Stir into cooking liquid; cook, uncovered, 10 minutes or until thickened.

6. Thinly slice steak against the grain. Return to slow cooker; cook 10 minutes or until thickened. Serve steak mixture on rolls.

sy party meatballs

makes 8 servings

**3 cups (1 pound 10 ounces) PREGO®
Marinara Italian Sauce**
1 jar (12 ounces) grape jelly
½ cup prepared chili sauce
**2½ pounds frozen fully-cooked meatballs,
cocktail size**

slow cooker directions

1. Stir the Italian Sauce, jelly, chili sauce and meatballs in a 4½-quart slow cooker.

2. Cover and cook on LOW for 6 to 7 hours* or until the meatballs are cooked through.

3. Serve the meatballs on a serving plate with toothpicks.

Or on HIGH for 3 to 4 hours.

prep time: 5 minutes • **cook time:** 6 to 7 hours

tip: For a special touch, serve with cranberry chutney for dipping.

moroccan spiced chicken wings

makes 8 servings

 ¼ **cup orange juice**
 3 tablespoons tomato paste
 2 teaspoons ground cumin
 1 teaspoon salt
 1 teaspoon curry powder
 1 teaspoon ground turmeric
 ½ **teaspoon ground cinnamon**
 ½ **teaspoon ground ginger**
 1 tablespoon olive oil
 5 pounds chicken wings, tips removed and split at joints

slow cooker directions

1. Combine orange juice, tomato paste, cumin, salt, curry powder, turmeric, cinnamon and ginger in large bowl.

2. Heat oil in large nonstick skillet over medium-high heat. Working in batches, cook wings 6 minutes or until browned. Transfer to bowl with sauce. Toss well to coat.

3. Place wings in slow cooker. Cover; cook on LOW 6 hours or on HIGH 3 hours.

prep time: 15 minutes • **cook time:** 6 hours (LOW) or 3 hours (HIGH)

bacon-wrapped fingerling potatoes with thyme
makes 4 to 6 servings

   1 pound fingerling potatoes
   2 tablespoons olive oil
   1 tablespoon minced fresh thyme, plus additional for garnish
   ½ teaspoon black pepper
   ¼ teaspoon paprika
   ½ pound bacon slices
   ¼ cup chicken broth

slow cooker directions

1. Toss potatoes, oil, 1 tablespoon thyme, pepper and paprika in large bowl.

2. Cut each bacon slice in half lengthwise. Wrap half slice bacon tightly around each potato.

3. Heat large skillet over medium heat; add potatoes. Reduce heat to medium-low; cook until lightly browned and bacon has tightened around potatoes.

4. Place potatoes in slow cooker; add broth. Cover; cook on HIGH 3 hours. Garnish with additional thyme.

prep time: 30 minutes • **cook time:** 3 hours

tip: This appetizer can be made even more eye-catching by using less common varieties of potatoes. Many interesting types of small potatoes can be found at farmers' markets. Purple potatoes, about the size of fingerling potatoes, can add unique flair to this dish.

bountiful beef

creamy beef stroganoff
makes 9 servings

- 2 cans (10¾ ounces each) CAMPBELL'S® Condensed Cream of Mushroom Soup
- ¼ cup water
- 2 tablespoons Worcestershire sauce
- 1 package (8 ounces) sliced white mushrooms
- 3 medium onions, coarsely chopped (about 1½ cups)
- 3 cloves garlic, minced
- ½ teaspoon ground black pepper
- 2 pounds boneless beef bottom round steaks, sliced diagonally into strips
- 1 cup sour cream
   Hot cooked egg noodles
   Chopped fresh parsley (optional)

slow cooker directions

1. Stir the soup, water, Worcestershire sauce, mushrooms, onions, garlic and black pepper in a 6-quart slow cooker. Add the beef and stir to coat.

2. Cover and cook on LOW for 8 to 9 hours* or until the beef is cooked through.

3. Stir the sour cream into the cooker. Serve with the egg noodles. Top with the parsley, if desired.

Or on HIGH for 4 to 5 hours.

kitchen tip: For more overall flavor and color, brown the beef before adding it to the slow cooker.

prep time: 15 minutes • **cook time:** 8 to 9 hours

shepherd's pie
makes 6 servings

1 pound ground beef
1 pound ground lamb
1 package (12 ounces) frozen chopped onions
2 teaspoons minced garlic
1 package (16 ounces) frozen peas and carrots
1 can (about 14 ounces) diced tomatoes, drained
3 tablespoons quick-cooking tapioca
2 teaspoons dried oregano
1 teaspoon salt
½ teaspoon black pepper
2 packages (24 ounces each) prepared mashed potatoes

slow cooker directions

1. Brown beef and lamb in large nonstick skillet over medium high heat 6 to 8 minutes, stirring to break up meat. Drain fat. Transfer to slow cooker.

2. Add onions and garlic to skillet. Cook and stir until onions begin to soften. Transfer to slow cooker.

3. Stir in peas and carrots, tomatoes, tapioca, oregano, salt and pepper. Cover; cook on LOW 7 to 8 hours.

4. Top with prepared mashed potatoes. Cover; cook 30 minutes or until potatoes are heated through.

beef chuck chili

makes 8 to 10 servings

3 tablespoons olive oil
5 pounds beef chuck roast
3 cups diced onions
4 poblano peppers, diced
2 serrano peppers,* diced
2 green bell peppers, diced
3 jalapeño peppers,* diced
2 tablespoons minced garlic
1 can (28 ounces) crushed tomatoes
4 ounces Mexican lager beer (optional)
¼ cup hot pepper sauce
1 tablespoon ground cumin
Black pepper
Corn bread

Hot peppers can sting and irritate the skin, so wear rubber gloves when handling peppers and do not touch your eyes.

slow cooker directions

1. Heat oil in large skillet over medium-high heat. Add roast; brown on all sides. Transfer to slow cooker.

2. Add onions, peppers and garlic to skillet; cook and stir 5 minutes or until onions are tender. Transfer to slow cooker. Stir in crushed tomatoes. Cover; cook on LOW 4 to 5 hours.

3. Shred beef. Stir in beer, if desired, hot pepper sauce and cumin. Season with black pepper. Serve over corn bread.

slow cooker asian short ribs

makes 4 to 6 servings

- ½ cup beef broth
- ¼ cup soy sauce
- ¼ cup dry sherry
- 1 tablespoon grated fresh ginger*
- 1 tablespoon honey
- 2 teaspoons minced garlic
- 3 pounds boneless beef short ribs
  Salt and black pepper
- ½ cup chopped green onions (optional)
  Hot cooked rice

To mince ginger quickly, cut a small chunk, remove the skin and put through a garlic press. Store remaining unpeeled ginger in a small resealable food storage bag in the refrigerator for up to 3 weeks.

slow cooker directions

1. Combine broth, soy sauce, sherry, ginger, honey and garlic in slow cooker.

2. Season short ribs with salt and pepper. Add to slow cooker, turning to coat all sides with sauce.

3. Cover; cook on LOW 7 to 8 hours.

4. Remove short ribs and place on serving dish. Garnish with green onions. Serve with rice.

picadillo
makes 8 servings

1½ **pounds ground beef**
2 **large onions, diced (about 2 cups)**
1¾ **cups SWANSON® Beef Stock**
1 **jar (8 ounces) PACE® Picante Sauce**
1 **tablespoon tomato paste**
1 **tablespoon chili powder**
1 **teaspoon ground cumin**
½ **cup raisins**
½ **cup toasted slivered almonds**
   Hot cooked rice

slow cooker directions

1. Cook the beef and onions in a 12-inch skillet over medium-high heat until the beef is well browned, stirring often to separate the meat. Pour off any fat.

2. Stir the beef mixture, stock, picante sauce, tomato paste, chili powder, cumin and raisins in a 6-quart slow cooker.

3. Cover and cook on LOW for 7 to 8 hours.* Top the beef mixture with the almonds. Serve with the rice.

Or on HIGH for 4 to 5 hours.

prep time: 15 minutes • **cook time:** 7 to 8 hours

swiss steak stew
makes 10 servings

- **4 pounds boneless beef top sirloin steaks**
- **2 cans (about 14 ounces each) diced tomatoes**
- **2 green bell peppers, cut into ½-inch strips**
- **2 onions, chopped**
- **1 tablespoon seasoned salt**
- **1 teaspoon black pepper**

slow cooker directions

1. Cut each steak into 4 pieces; place in slow cooker. Add tomatoes, bell peppers and onions. Sprinkle with seasoned salt and black pepper.

2. Cover; cook on LOW 8 hours or until beef is tender.

tip: To increase the flavor of the finished dish and more closely follow the traditional preparation of Swiss steak, dust the steak pieces with flour and brown in a bit of olive oil in a large skillet over medium-high heat before adding them to the slow cooker.

spicy sausage bolognese sauce

makes 6 servings

      1 pound ground beef
      1 pound hot Italian sausage, casings removed
      1 tablespoon olive oil
   ¼ pound pancetta, diced
      1 onion, finely diced
      2 carrots, peeled and finely diced
      1 stalk celery, finely diced
   ½ teaspoon salt
   ½ teaspoon black pepper
      3 tablespoons tomato paste
      1 tablespoon minced garlic
      2 cans (28 ounces each) diced tomatoes, drained
   ¾ cup whole milk
   ¾ cup dry red wine
      1 pound hot cooked spaghetti
         Grated Parmesan cheese (optional)

slow cooker directions

1. Brown ground beef and sausage in large skillet over medium-high heat 6 to 8 minutes, stirring to break up meat. Transfer to slow cooker.

2. Add oil to skillet; heat over medium heat. Add pancetta; cook until crisp and brown, stirring occasionally. Transfer to slow cooker.

3. Add onion, carrots, celery, salt and pepper to skillet; cook and stir until tender. Add tomato paste and garlic; cook and stir 1 minute. Transfer to slow cooker. Stir in tomatoes, milk and wine.

4. Cover; cook on LOW 6 hours. Reserve 5 cups sauce for another use. Toss remaining 6 cups sauce with spaghetti and sprinkle with Parmesan cheese, if desired, just before serving.

asian beef with mandarin oranges
makes 6 servings

    2 tablespoons vegetable oil
    2 pounds boneless beef chuck, cut into ½-inch strips
    1 onion, thinly sliced
    1 green bell pepper, sliced
    1 package (about 3 ounces) shiitake mushrooms, sliced
    1 bunch bok choy, chopped
    1 can (5 ounces) sliced water chestnuts, drained
    ⅓ cup soy sauce
    2 teaspoons minced fresh ginger
    ¼ teaspoon salt
    2 tablespoons cornstarch
    1 can (11 ounces) mandarin oranges, drained and syrup reserved
    2 cups beef broth
    6 cups steamed rice

slow cooker directions

1. Heat oil in large skillet over medium-high heat. Working in batches, brown beef on all sides. Transfer to slow cooker.

2. Add onion to skillet; cook and stir over medium heat until softened. Add green pepper, mushrooms, bok choy, water chestnuts, soy sauce, ginger and salt; cook and stir 5 minutes or until bok choy is wilted. Spoon mixture over beef.

3. Whisk cornstarch into reserved mandarin orange syrup in medium bowl until smooth. Stir in broth; pour into slow cooker. Cover; cook on LOW 10 hours or on HIGH 5 hours.

4. Stir in mandarin oranges. Serve over rice.

prep time: 25 minutes • **cook time:** 10 hours (LOW) or 5 hours (HIGH)

braised short ribs with red wine tomato sauce

makes 8 servings

4 pounds beef short ribs, cut into serving-size pieces
2⅔ cups **PREGO®** Fresh Mushroom Italian Sauce
1 cup dry red wine
1 bag fresh or frozen whole baby carrots
1 large onion, chopped (about 1 cup)
   Hot cooked rice

slow cooker directions

1. Season the ribs as desired.

2. Stir the Italian Sauce, wine, carrots and onion in a 3½-quart slow cooker. Add the ribs and turn to coat.

3. Cover and cook on LOW for 7 to 8 hours* or until the ribs are fork-tender. Serve with the rice.

Or on HIGH for 4 to 5 hours.

prep time: 10 minutes • **cook time:** 7 to 8 hours

tip: Short ribs are a less tender cut that need moist heat cooking. After long, slow cooking, they are juicy and delicious. If you are using bone-in short ribs for this recipe, be sure to have your butcher cut them into serving-size pieces because it is difficult to do yourself.

veal pot roast
makes 4 to 6 servings

2 tablespoons olive oil
1 veal shoulder roast (2½ pounds)
    Salt and black pepper
2 cloves garlic, slivered
¾ pound pearl onions, peeled (see Note)
½ cup sliced fennel
1 package (3½ ounces) shiitake mushrooms,
    wiped clean and sliced
6 plum tomatoes, quartered
2 cups chicken broth
1 cup light beer
1 teaspoon minced fresh herbs (rosemary leaves,
    thyme and sage)
¼ teaspoon red pepper flakes
¼ teaspoon grated lemon peel

slow cooker directions

1. Heat oil in large skillet over medium-high heat. Poke holes about 1 inch deep all over roast with paring knife. Place one garlic sliver into each hole. Season roast with salt and pepper; brown on all sides. Transfer to slow cooker.

2. Add onions, fennel, mushrooms and tomatoes to slow cooker. Pour broth and beer over roast. Sprinkle herbs, red pepper flakes and lemon peel over roast.

3. Cover; cook on LOW 8 to 10 hours. Remove roast from slow cooker; let stand 10 minutes. Slice roast. Serve with sauce and vegetables.

note: To peel pearl onions, place in a large pot of boiling water and cook 1 minute. Drain well and run under cold water to cool slightly. Rub lightly, if necessary. The skins should come off easily.

easy beef burgundy
makes 4 to 6 servings

1½ **pounds beef round steak or beef stew meat, cut into 1-inch pieces**
1 **can (10¾ ounces) condensed cream of mushroom soup, undiluted**
1 **cup red wine**
1 **onion, chopped**
1 **can (4 ounces) sliced mushrooms, drained**
1 **package (1 ounce) dry onion soup mix**
1 **tablespoon minced garlic**

slow cooker directions

1. Combine beef, soup, wine, onion, mushrooms, soup mix and garlic in slow cooker; stir well.

2. Cover; cook on LOW 6 to 8 hours.

tip: This savory beef is perfect for serving over hot cooked noodles, rice or mashed potatoes, all of which will absorb any of the extra sauce, creating an even heartier dish. You can also add chopped vegetables such as carrots or parsnips to the slow cooker with the beef to round out the meal.

swiss steak delight
makes 6 servings

1 boneless beef round steak (about
   1½ pounds), cut into 6 pieces
½ pound new potatoes, cut into quarters
1½ cups fresh or frozen whole baby carrots
1 medium onion, sliced (about ½ cup)
1 can (14½ ounces) diced tomatoes with
   Italian herbs
1 can (10¼ ounces) CAMPBELL'S® Beef
   Gravy

slow cooker directions

1. Cook the beef in 2 batches in a 12-inch nonstick skillet over medium-high heat until well browned on both sides.

2. Place the potatoes, carrots, onion and beef into a 3½-quart slow cooker. Stir the tomatoes and gravy in a medium bowl. Pour the gravy mixture over the beef and vegetables.

3. Cover and cook on LOW for 8 to 9 hours* or until the beef is fork-tender.

Or on HIGH for 4 to 5 hours.

prep time: 15 minutes • **cook time:** 8 to 9 hours

ginger beef with peppers and mushrooms

makes 6 servings

1½ pounds beef top round steak, cut into ¾-inch cubes
24 baby carrots
 1 red bell pepper, chopped
 1 green bell pepper, chopped
 1 onion, chopped
 1 package (8 ounces) mushrooms, halved
 1 cup reduced-sodium beef broth
½ cup hoisin sauce
¼ cup quick-cooking tapioca
 2 tablespoons grated fresh ginger
   Hot cooked rice

slow cooker directions

1. Combine beef, carrots, bell peppers, onion, mushrooms, broth, hoisin sauce, tapioca and ginger in slow cooker.

2. Cover; cook on LOW 8 to 9 hours. Serve over rice.

tip: Tapioca, derived from the root of the cassava plant, is a starch that acts as a thickener in this recipe, creating a rich sauce that coats the beef and vegetables.

spanish paella with chicken and sausage
makes 4 servings

- **1 tablespoon olive oil**
- **4 chicken thighs**
- **1 onion, chopped**
- **1 clove garlic, minced**
- **4 cups chicken broth**
- **1 pound hot smoked sausage, sliced into rounds**
- **1 can (about 14 ounces) stewed tomatoes, undrained**
- **1 cup uncooked arborio rice**
- **1 pinch saffron (optional)**
- **½ cup frozen peas, thawed**

slow cooker directions

1. Heat oil in large skillet over medium-high heat. Add chicken; brown on all sides. Transfer to slow cooker.

2. Add onion to skillet; cook and stir 5 minutes or until translucent. Add garlic; cook and stir 30 seconds. Stir in broth, sausage, tomatoes, rice and saffron, if desired. Pour over chicken.

3. Cover; cook on LOW 6 hours or on HIGH 3 hours.

4. Remove chicken to serving platter. Fluff rice with fork. Stir in peas. Spoon rice onto platter with chicken.

prep time: 15 minutes • **cook time:** 6 hours (LOW) or 3 hours (HIGH)

chicken vesuvio
makes 4 to 6 servings

      3 tablespoons all-purpose flour
  1½ teaspoons dried oregano
      1 teaspoon salt
   ½ teaspoon black pepper
      1 whole chicken (3 to 4 pounds), cut up
      2 tablespoons olive oil
      4 baking potatoes, cut into wedges
      2 onions, cut into thin wedges
      4 cloves garlic, minced
   ¼ cup chicken broth
   ¼ cup dry white wine
   ¼ cup chopped fresh Italian parsley
         Lemon wedges (optional)

slow cooker directions

1. Combine flour, oregano, salt and pepper in large resealable food storage bag. Add several pieces of chicken to bag; shake to coat. Repeat with remaining chicken.

2. Heat oil in large skillet over medium heat. Add chicken; cook 10 to 12 minutes or until browned on all sides, turning occasionally.

3. Place potatoes, onions and garlic in slow cooker. Add broth and wine. Top with chicken; pour accumulated juices from skillet over chicken.

4. Cover; cook on LOW 6 to 7 hours or on HIGH 3 to 3½ hours.

5. Serve chicken and vegetables with juices from slow cooker. Sprinkle with parsley. Garnish with lemon wedges.

curried turkey cutlets

makes 8 servings

2 cans (10¾ ounces each) **CAMPBELL'S®** Condensed Cream
of Chicken Soup (Regular or 98% Fat Free)

2 tablespoons water

1 tablespoon curry powder

½ teaspoon cracked black pepper

8 turkey breast cutlets (about 2 pounds)

¼ cup heavy cream

½ cup seedless red grapes, cut in half

Hot cooked rice or seasoned rice blend

slow cooker directions

1. Stir the soup, water, curry powder and black pepper in a 3½ to 4-quart slow cooker. Add the turkey and turn to coat.

2. Cover and cook on LOW for 6 to 7 hours* or until the turkey is cooked through.

3. Stir the cream and grapes into the cooker. Serve with the rice.

Or on HIGH for 3 to 4 hours.

kitchen tip: This recipe is delicious served with a variety of toppers, including chutney, toasted coconut, sliced almonds and/or raisins.

prep time: 10 minutes • **cook time:** 6 to 7 hours

hoisin barbecue chicken thighs
makes 6 to 8 servings

- ⅔ cup hoisin sauce
- ⅓ cup barbecue sauce
- 3 tablespoons quick-cooking tapioca
- 1 tablespoon sugar
- 1 tablespoon reduced-sodium soy sauce
- ¼ teaspoon red pepper flakes
- 12 bone-in chicken thighs, skinned (3½ to 4 pounds total)
- 1½ pounds uncooked ramen noodles or spaghetti
  Sliced green onions (optional)

slow cooker directions

1. Combine hoisin sauce, barbecue sauce, tapioca, sugar, soy sauce and red pepper flakes in slow cooker. Add chicken, meat side down.

2. Cover; cook on LOW 8 to 9 hours.

3. Just before serving, cook noodles according to package directions. Serve chicken over noodles. Garnish with green onions.

chicken cordon bleu
makes 4 servings

- ¼ cup all-purpose flour
- 1 teaspoon paprika
- ½ teaspoon salt
- ¼ teaspoon black pepper
- 4 boneless chicken breasts, lightly pounded*
- 4 slices ham
- 4 slices Swiss cheese
- 2 tablespoons olive oil
- ½ cup white wine
- ½ cup chicken broth
- 2 tablespoons cornstarch
- ½ cup half-and-half

*Place chicken between 2 pieces of plastic wrap and pound with back of skillet to flatten.

slow cooker directions

1. Combine flour, paprika, salt and pepper in large resealable food storage bag; shake well.

2. Place chicken on cutting board, skin side down. Place 1 slice ham and 1 slice Swiss cheese on each piece. Fold chicken up to enclose filling and secure with toothpick. Place in bag with seasoned flour and shake gently to coat.

3. Heat oil in large skillet over medium-high heat. Add chicken; brown on all sides. Transfer to slow cooker.

4. Add wine to skillet, stirring to scrape up browned bits. Pour into slow cooker; add broth. Cover; cook on LOW 2 hours.

5. Remove chicken; keep warm. Whisk cornstarch into half-and-half in small bowl until smooth. Stir into cooking liquid. Cover; cook 15 minutes or until sauce is thickened. Remove toothpicks from chicken before serving.

turkey fajita wraps
makes 8 servings

2 cups PACE® Picante Sauce
2 large green or red bell peppers, cut into
    2-inch-long strips (about 4 cups)
1½ cups frozen whole kernel corn, thawed
2 tablespoons lime juice
1 tablespoon chili powder
3 cloves garlic, minced
2 pounds turkey breast cutlets, cut into
    4-inch-long strips
16 flour tortillas (8-inch), warmed
    Shredded Mexican cheese blend

slow cooker directions

1. Stir the picante sauce, bell peppers, corn, lime juice, chili powder, garlic and turkey in a 4-quart slow cooker.

2. Cover and cook on LOW for 6 to 7 hours* or until the turkey is cooked through.

3. Spoon about ½ cup of the turkey mixture down the center of each tortilla. Top with the cheese. Fold the tortillas around the filling.

Or on HIGH for 3 to 4 hours.

kitchen tip: This dish is delicious served with an assortment of additional toppers such as sliced green onions, sliced black olives, shredded lettuce, sliced jalapeño peppers, sour cream and/or chopped fresh cilantro.

prep time: 10 minutes • **cook time:** 6 to 7 hours

country chicken and vegetables with creamy herb sauce

makes 4 servings

1 pound new potatoes, cut into ½-inch wedges
1 onion, cut into 8 wedges
½ cup coarsely chopped celery
4 bone-in chicken drumsticks, skinned
4 bone-in chicken thighs, skinned
1 can (10¾ ounces) condensed cream of chicken soup, undiluted
1 envelope (1 ounce) dry ranch dressing mix
½ teaspoon dried thyme
¼ teaspoon black pepper
½ cup whipping cream
Salt (optional)
¼ cup finely chopped green onions (optional)

slow cooker directions

1. Coat slow cooker with nonstick cooking spray. Place potatoes, onion and celery in bottom. Top with chicken.

2. Combine soup, dressing mix, thyme and pepper in small bowl. Spoon mixture evenly over chicken and vegetables. Cover; cook on HIGH 3½ hours.

3. Transfer chicken to shallow serving bowl with slotted spoon. Stir cream into cooking liquid. Season with salt, if desired. Pour sauce over chicken. Garnish with green onions.

note: To skin chicken easily, grasp skin with paper towel and pull away. Repeat with fresh paper towel for each piece of chicken, discarding skins and towels.

prep time: 20 minutes • **cook time:** 3½ hours

chicken cacciatore
makes 6 to 8 servings

- ¼ cup vegetable oil
- 2½ to 3 pounds chicken tenders, cut into bite-size pieces
- 1 can (28 ounces) crushed Italian-style tomatoes
- 2 cans (8 ounces each) tomato sauce
- 1 onion, chopped
- 1 can (4 ounces) sliced mushrooms, drained
- 2 cloves garlic, minced
- 1 teaspoon salt
- 1 teaspoon dried oregano
- ½ teaspoon dried thyme
- ½ teaspoon black pepper
- Hot cooked spaghetti

slow cooker directions

1. Heat oil in large skillet over medium-low heat. Brown chicken on all sides. Transfer to slow cooker.

2. Stir tomatoes, tomato sauce, onion, mushrooms, garlic, salt, oregano, thyme and pepper into slow cooker.

3. Cover; cook on LOW 6 to 8 hours. Serve over spaghetti.

indian-style apricot chicken
makes 4 to 6 servings

6 chicken thighs
   Salt and black pepper
1 tablespoon vegetable oil
1 onion, chopped
2 tablespoons grated fresh ginger
2 cloves garlic, minced
½ teaspoon ground cinnamon
⅛ teaspoon ground allspice
1 can (about 14 ounces) diced tomatoes
1 cup chicken broth
1 package (8 ounces) dried apricots
1 pinch saffron (optional)
   Hot basmati rice
2 tablespoons chopped fresh Italian parsley (optional)

slow cooker directions

1. Coat slow cooker with nonstick cooking spray. Season chicken with salt and pepper. Heat oil in large skillet over medium-high heat. Brown chicken on all sides. Transfer to slow cooker.

2. Add onion to skillet; cook and stir 5 minutes or until translucent. Stir in ginger, garlic, cinnamon and allspice; cook 15 to 30 seconds or until fragrant. Add tomatoes and broth; cook 2 to 3 minutes or until heated through. Pour into slow cooker.

3. Add apricots and saffron, if desired. Cover; cook on LOW 6 hours or on HIGH 3 hours. Serve with rice and garnish with parsley.

prep time: 15 minutes • **cook time:** 6 hours (LOW) or 3 hours (HIGH)

turkey paprikash
makes 4 servings

   3 tablespoons all-purpose flour
¼ teaspoon salt
¼ teaspoon black pepper
   1 pound turkey breast, cut into bite-size pieces
   2 tablespoons butter, divided
   1 onion, chopped
   1 tablespoon sweet paprika
½ cup chicken broth
12 ounces noodles
¼ cup whipping cream
¼ cup sour cream

slow cooker directions

1. Place flour, salt and pepper in large resealable food storage bag. Add turkey and shake well to coat.

2. Melt 1 tablespoon butter in large skillet over medium-high heat. Add turkey in single layer. Brown on all sides. Place turkey in single layer in slow cooker.

3. Melt remaining 1 tablespoon butter in skillet over medium-high heat. Add onion; cook and stir 2 minutes or until golden brown. Stir in paprika and cook 30 seconds. Add broth, stirring to scrape up browned bits. Transfer to slow cooker. Cover; cook on LOW 1 hour.

4. Meanwhile, cook noodles until tender. Drain and place in large shallow bowl.

5. Combine whipping cream and sour cream in small bowl. Stir in ½ cup cooking liquid from slow cooker. Stir into slow cooker. Cover; cook on LOW 5 minutes. Serve turkey and sauce over noodles.

sweet and sour chicken
makes 4 servings

   ¼ **cup chicken broth**
   2 **tablespoons soy sauce**
   2 **tablespoons hoisin sauce**
   1 **tablespoon cider vinegar**
   1 **tablespoon tomato paste**
   2 **teaspoons packed brown sugar**
   1 **clove garlic, minced**
   ¼ **teaspoon black pepper**
   1 **pound boneless skinless chicken thighs, cut into 1-inch pieces**
   2 **teaspoons cornstarch**
   2 **tablespoons minced fresh chives**
      Hot cooked rice

slow cooker directions

1. Combine broth, soy sauce, hoisin sauce, vinegar, tomato paste, brown sugar, garlic and pepper in slow cooker; stir well.

2. Add chicken and stir. Cover; cook on LOW 2½ to 3½ hours. Remove chicken with slotted spoon; keep warm.

3. Whisk cornstarch into 2 tablespoons cooking liquid in small bowl until smooth. Add to slow cooker. Stir in chives.

4. *Turn slow cooker to HIGH.* Cook, uncovered, 2 minutes or until sauce is slightly thickened, stirring constantly. Serve chicken and sauce over rice.

prep time: 10 minutes • **cook time:** 2½ to 3½ hours

chicken with artichoke-parmesan dressing

makes 6 servings

2 cans (about 14 ounces each) quartered artichoke hearts, drained and coarsely chopped

4 ounces herb-seasoned stuffing mix

1½ cups frozen seasoning blend vegetables, thawed*

¾ cup plus 1 tablespoon grated Parmesan cheese, divided

¾ cup mayonnaise

1 egg, beaten

½ teaspoon salt

½ teaspoon dried oregano

½ teaspoon paprika

¼ teaspoon black pepper

6 bone-in chicken breasts (about 3½ pounds)

*Seasoning blend vegetables are a mixture of chopped bell peppers, onions and celery. If you are unable to find frozen vegetables, use ½ cup each of these fresh vegetables.

slow cooker directions

1. Lightly coat slow cooker with nonstick cooking spray. Combine artichokes, stuffing, vegetables, ¾ cup Parmesan cheese, mayonnaise and egg in large bowl until well blended. Transfer mixture to slow cooker.

2. Combine salt, oregano, paprika and pepper in small bowl. Rub evenly onto chicken. Arrange chicken on top of artichoke mixture in slow cooker, overlapping slightly. Cover; cook on HIGH 3 hours.

3. Transfer chicken to serving platter. Cover with foil to keep warm. Stir artichoke mixture in slow cooker. Sprinkle evenly with remaining 1 tablespoon Parmesan cheese. Cook, uncovered, 20 minutes or until thickened. Serve dressing with chicken.

greek chicken pitas with creamy mustard sauce

makes 4 servings

1 green bell pepper, cut into ½-inch strips
1 onion, cut into 8 wedges
1 pound boneless skinless chicken breasts
1 tablespoon extra virgin olive oil
2 teaspoons Greek seasoning
½ teaspoon salt, divided
¼ cup plain yogurt
¼ cup mayonnaise
1 tablespoon prepared mustard
4 pita bread rounds
½ cup crumbled feta cheese
   Toppings: sliced cucumbers, sliced tomatoes,
     kalamata olives

slow cooker directions

1. Coat slow cooker with nonstick cooking spray. Place bell pepper and onion in bottom. Add chicken and drizzle with oil. Sprinkle with seasoning and ¼ teaspoon salt.

2. Cover; cook on HIGH 1¾ hours or until chicken is no longer pink in center (vegetables will be slightly crisp-tender).

3. Remove chicken and slice. Remove vegetables using slotted spoon.

4. Combine yogurt, mayonnaise, mustard and remaining ¼ teaspoon salt in small bowl. Stir until blended.

5. Warm pitas according to package directions. Cut in half and fill pockets with chicken, yogurt sauce, vegetables and feta cheese. Add desired toppings.

prep time: 10 minutes • **cook time:** 1¾ hours

ham with spiced cola sauce
makes 10 to 12 servings

- 1¼ **cups packed dark brown sugar, divided**
- ¾ **cup cola, divided**
- 3 **tablespoons cider vinegar**
- 1 **tablespoon plus 1½ teaspoons grated orange peel**
- 2 **teaspoons ground cinnamon**
- 1 **teaspoon ground allspice**
- 6 **whole cloves**
- ¼ **teaspoon red pepper flakes**
- 1 **fully cooked bone-in ham (about 6 pounds)**
- 2 **tablespoons cornstarch**

slow cooker directions

1. Lightly coat slow cooker with nonstick cooking spray. Add 1 cup brown sugar, ½ cup cola, vinegar, orange peel, cinnamon, allspice, cloves and red pepper flakes; whisk until well blended. Place ham in slow cooker, cut side up.

2. Cover; cook on LOW 5 hours or until ham is slightly separated from bone. Transfer ham to cutting board. Cover and let stand 20 minutes.

3. Meanwhile, strain drippings into large measuring cup. Let stand 5 minutes; skim and discard solids. Return drippings to slow cooker. Stir in remaining ¼ cup brown sugar.

4. *Turn slow cooker to HIGH.* Stir remaining ¼ cup cola into cornstarch in small bowl until smooth. Whisk into slow cooker. Cover; cook 20 minutes or until thickened. Serve sauce with ham.

panama pork stew
makes 6 servings

    2 small sweet potatoes (about ¾ pound), peeled and cut into 2-inch pieces
    1 package (10 ounces) frozen corn
    1 package (9 ounces) frozen cut green beans
    1 cup chopped onion
  1¼ pounds pork stew meat, cut into 1-inch cubes
    1 can (about 14 ounces) diced tomatoes
    ¼ cup water
    1 to 2 tablespoons chili powder
    ½ teaspoon salt
    ½ teaspoon ground coriander

slow cooker directions

1. Place sweet potatoes, corn, green beans and onion in slow cooker. Top with pork.

2. Combine tomatoes, water, chili powder, salt and coriander in medium bowl. Pour over pork in slow cooker.

3. Cover; cook on LOW 7 to 9 hours.

prep time: 10 minutes • **cook time:** 7 to 9 hours

seared pork roast with currant cherry salsa

makes 6 servings

1½ teaspoons chili powder
¾ teaspoon salt
½ teaspoon garlic powder
½ teaspoon paprika
¼ teaspoon ground allspice
1 boneless pork loin roast (2 pounds)
Nonstick cooking spray
½ cup water
1 pound bag frozen pitted dark cherries, thawed, drained and halved
¼ cup currants or dark raisins
1 teaspoon balsamic vinegar
1 teaspoon grated orange peel
⅛ to ¼ teaspoon red pepper flakes

slow cooker directions

1. Combine chili powder, salt, garlic powder, paprika and allspice in small bowl. Coat roast evenly with spice mixture, pressing to adhere.

2. Spray large skillet with cooking spray; heat over medium-high heat. Brown roast on all sides. Transfer to slow cooker.

3. Pour water into skillet, stirring to scrape up browned bits. Pour into slow cooker around roast. Cover; cook on LOW 6 to 8 hours or until pork reaches 160°F. (For tenderness, do not cook on HIGH.)

4. Remove roast from slow cooker. Tent with foil; keep warm. Strain juices from slow cooker; discard solids. Pour juice into small saucepan; keep warm over low heat.

5. *Turn slow cooker to HIGH.* Add cherries, currants, vinegar, orange peel and red pepper flakes. Cover; cook 30 minutes. Slice pork and spoon warm juices over meat. Serve with salsa.

shredded pork wraps
makes 6 servings

1 cup salsa, divided
2 tablespoons cornstarch
1 boneless pork loin roast (2 pounds)
6 (8-inch) flour tortillas
3 cups broccoli slaw mix
½ cup shredded Cheddar cheese

slow cooker directions

1. Combine ¼ cup salsa and cornstarch in small bowl; stir until smooth. Pour mixture into slow cooker.

2. Top with pork roast. Pour remaining ¾ cup salsa over roast. Cover; cook on LOW 6 to 8 hours.

3. Transfer roast to cutting board. Trim and discard fat from pork. Pull pork into coarse shreds using two forks.

4. Divide shredded meat evenly among tortillas. Spoon about 2 tablespoons salsa mixture on top of meat in each tortilla. Top evenly with broccoli slaw and cheese. Fold bottom edge of tortilla over filling; fold in sides. Roll up completely to enclose filling.

5. Serve remaining salsa mixture as dipping sauce.

prep time: 5 minutes • **cook time:** 6 to 8 hours

tip: Broccoli slaw mix is a delicious alternative to cabbage-based coleslaw mixes. Found in the pre-washed salad section of the grocery store, this nutritious mix is made from shredded broccoli stems and carrots.

lemon pork chops
makes 4 servings

   1 tablespoon vegetable oil
   4 boneless pork chops
   3 cans (about 8 ounces each) tomato
       sauce
   1 onion, quartered and sliced
   1 green bell pepper, cut into strips
   1 tablespoon lemon-pepper seasoning
   1 tablespoon Worcestershire sauce
   2 lemons, quartered, divided

slow cooker directions

1. Heat oil in large skillet over medium heat. Brown pork chops on both sides. Transfer to slow cooker.

2. Combine tomato sauce, onion, bell pepper, lemon-pepper seasoning and Worcestershire sauce in medium bowl. Add to slow cooker.

3. Squeeze juice from 4 lemon quarters over mixture; place squeezed lemon quarters into slow cooker. Cover; cook on LOW 6 to 8 hours. Remove and discard cooked lemon before serving. Serve pork with remaining 4 lemon quarters.

serving suggestion: These pork chops are great served with green beans and couscous.

prep time: 10 minutes • **cook time:** 6 to 8 hours

slow cooked pork & sauerkraut
makes 6 servings

> 2 jars (32 ounces each) sauerkraut, rinsed and drained
> 2½ cups water
> 3 tablespoons brown mustard
> 1 package (about 1 ounce) dry onion soup mix
> 3 pounds boneless pork loin roast

slow cooker directions

1. Combine sauerkraut, water, mustard and soup mix in slow cooker; mix well. Add pork to slow cooker.

2. Cover; cook on LOW 8 hours.

3. Slice pork; serve with sauerkraut.

prep time: 5 minutes • **cook time:** 8 hours

tip: Sauerkraut, a traditional fermented or preserved cabbage most commonly associated with the German culinary tradition, has a distinctive flavor and pungent aroma. As such, this recipe calls for rinsing and draining it instead of serving it as packaged. This helps to dilute the salt and spices used to season the cabbage and to prevent the trademark tanginess of the sauerkraut from overwhelming the other flavors in the dish.

posole
makes 8 servings

3 pounds boneless pork shoulder, trimmed of fat and cubed
3 cans (about 14 ounces each) white hominy, drained
¾ cup chili sauce

slow cooker directions

1. Combine all ingredients in slow cooker.

2. Cover; cook on HIGH 5 hours.

3. *Turn slow cooker to LOW.* Cover; cook 10 hours or until pork is fork-tender.

tip: Hominy consists of dried corn kernels, typically made from white or yellow varieties, that have been stripped of their hull and germ either chemically, through treatment with lye or slaked lime, or mechanically. Thanks to this ingenious method for extending the shelf life of this staple food, hominy can be served whole in dishes such as this rich and satisfying posole, ground into grits, or transformed into masa, the soft dough that serves as the foundation of the tortillas and arepas popular throughout Latin American cooking.

pork tenderloin with thyme and white beans

makes 10 to 12 servings

2 to 3 pork tenderloins (1 to 2 pounds each) *or* **1 boneless pork top loin roast (3 to 4 pounds)**
1 head garlic, peeled and separated into individual cloves
   Salt and white pepper
2 cups dried navy beans, sorted, rinsed and soaked overnight
1 cup red wine
¾ cup white wine
¼ cup hot water
2 tablespoons dried thyme
2 teaspoons dried oregano
1 teaspoon chopped garlic
1 teaspoon baking soda
2 yellow onions, quartered
1 leek, cut into ⅛-inch-thick slices
1 tablespoon olive oil
1 tablespoon butter, melted

slow cooker directions

1. Poke holes about 1 inch deep all over pork with paring knife. Place one garlic clove into each hole. Season with salt and white pepper.

2. Drain beans; place in slow cooker. Add red wine, white wine, water, thyme, oregano, chopped garlic and baking soda; mix well. Top with onions, leek and pork. Combine oil and butter; pour over pork.

3. Cover; cook on LOW for 6 to 8 hours.

chili verde
makes 4 to 8 servings

1 tablespoon vegetable oil
1 to 2 pounds boneless pork chops
   Sliced carrots (enough to cover bottom of slow cooker)
1 jar (24 ounces) mild green salsa
   Chopped onion (optional)

slow cooker directions

1. Heat oil in large skillet over medium-low heat. Brown pork on both sides. Drain fat.

2. Place carrots in bottom of slow cooker. Add pork; pour salsa over top. Sprinkle with onion, if desired.

3. Cover; cook on HIGH 6 to 8 hours.

prep time: 10 minutes • **cook time:** 6 to 8 hours

tip: You can also shred this delicious pork and serve it on corn tortillas with assorted toppings for a variation on taco night.

golden harvest pork stew
makes 4 servings

- **1 pound boneless pork cutlets, cut into 1-inch pieces**
- **2 tablespoons all-purpose flour, divided**
- **1 tablespoon vegetable oil**
- **2 medium Yukon Gold potatoes, unpeeled and cut into 1-inch cubes**
- **1 large sweet potato, peeled and cut into 1-inch cubes**
- **1 cup chopped carrots**
- **1 ear corn, broken into 4 pieces** *or* **½ cup corn kernels**
- **½ cup chicken broth**
- **1 jalapeño pepper,* seeded and finely chopped**
- **1 clove garlic, minced**
- **1 teaspoon salt**
- **¼ teaspoon black pepper**
- **¼ teaspoon dried thyme**

*Jalapeño peppers can sting and irritate the skin, so wear rubber gloves when handling peppers and do not touch your eyes.

slow cooker directions

1. Toss pork with 1 tablespoon flour. Heat oil in large nonstick skillet over medium-high heat; brown pork on all sides. Transfer to slow cooker.

2. Add potatoes, sweet potato, carrots, corn, broth, jalapeño pepper, garlic, salt, black pepper and thyme. Cover; cook on LOW 5 to 6 hours.

3. *Turn slow cooker to HIGH.* Whisk remaining 1 tablespoon flour into ¼ cup cooking liquid in small bowl until smooth. Stir into stew. Cook, uncovered, 10 minutes or until thickened.

cuban pork sandwiches
makes 8 servings

Nonstick cooking spray
1 pork loin roast (about 2 pounds)
½ cup orange juice
2 tablespoons lime juice
1 tablespoon minced garlic
1½ teaspoons salt
½ teaspoon red pepper flakes
2 tablespoons yellow mustard
8 crusty bread rolls, split in half
(about 6 inches each)
8 slices Swiss cheese
8 thin ham slices
4 small dill pickles, thinly sliced lengthwise

slow cooker directions

1. Coat slow cooker with cooking spray; add pork loin.

2. Combine orange juice, lime juice, garlic, salt and red pepper flakes in small bowl. Pour over pork.

3. Cover; cook on LOW 7 hours or on HIGH 3½ hours. Transfer pork to cutting board and allow to cool. Cut into thin slices.

4. To serve, spread mustard on cut sides of rolls. Divide pork slices among roll bottoms. Top with one slice each of Swiss cheese, ham and pickle. Cover with top of roll.

5. Coat large skillet with cooking spray; heat over medium heat. Working in batches, arrange sandwiches in skillet. Cover with foil and top with dinner plate to press down sandwiches. (If necessary, weigh down with 2 to 3 cans to compress sandwiches lightly.) Heat until cheese is melted.* Serve immediately.

*Or use tabletop grill to compress and heat sandwiches.

prep time: 10 minutes • **cook time:** 7 hours (LOW) or 3½ hours (HIGH)

rio grande ribs
makes 6 servings

4 pounds country-style pork ribs, trimmed of all visible fat
Salt
Black pepper
1 jar (16 ounces) picante sauce
½ cup beer, nonalcoholic malt beverage or beef broth
¼ cup FRANK'S® REDHOT® Cayenne Pepper Sauce
1 teaspoon chili powder
2 cups FRENCH'S® French Fried Onions

slow cooker directions

1. Season ribs with salt and pepper. Broil ribs 6 inches from heat on rack in broiler pan for 10 minutes or until well-browned, turning once. Place ribs in slow cooker. Combine picante sauce, beer, FRANK'S® REDHOT® Cayenne Pepper Sauce and chili powder in small bowl. Pour mixture over top.

2. Cover and cook on LOW for 6 hours or on HIGH for 3 hours or until ribs are tender. Transfer ribs to serving platter; keep warm. Skim fat from liquid.

3. Turn slow cooker to HIGH. Add 1 cup FRENCH'S® French Fried Onions to the stoneware. Cook 10 to 15 minutes or until slightly thickened. Spoon sauce over ribs and sprinkle with remaining 1 cup French Fried Onions. Splash on more FRANK'S® REDHOT® Cayenne Pepper Sauce to taste.

spicy citrus pork with pineapple salsa
makes 4 to 6 servings

- 1½ teaspoons ground cumin
- ½ teaspoon black pepper
- ¼ teaspoon salt
- 1½ pounds center-cut pork loin
- 1 tablespoon vegetable oil
- 2 cans (8 ounces each) pineapple tidbits* in juice, drained, juice reserved
- 2 tablespoons lemon juice, divided
- ½ cup finely chopped orange or red bell pepper
- 2 tablespoons finely chopped red onion
- 1 tablespoon chopped fresh cilantro or mint
- 1 teaspoon grated lemon peel
- ½ teaspoon grated fresh ginger
- ⅛ teaspoon red pepper flakes (optional)

*If tidbits are unavailable, purchase pineapple chunks and coarsely chop.

slow cooker directions

1. Coat slow cooker with nonstick cooking spray. Combine cumin, black pepper and salt in small bowl. Rub evenly onto pork. Heat oil in medium skillet over medium-high heat; brown pork on all sides. Transfer to slow cooker.

2. Spoon 2 tablespoons reserved pineapple juice and 1 tablespoon lemon juice over pork. Cover; cook on LOW 2 hours or on HIGH 1 hour or until meat thermometer registers 160°F and pork is barely pink in center.

3. Meanwhile, toss pineapple, remaining 2 tablespoons pineapple juice, 1 tablespoon lemon juice, bell pepper, onion, cilantro, lemon peel, ginger and red pepper flakes, if desired, in medium bowl.

4. Transfer pork to serving platter. Let stand 10 minutes before slicing. Pour juices evenly over pork. Serve with salsa.

prep time: 15 minutes • **cook time:** 2 hours (LOW) or 1 hour (HIGH)

chorizo and corn dressing
makes 4 to 6 servings

½ pound chorizo sausage, removed from casings
1 can (about 14 ounces) reduced-sodium chicken broth
1 can (10¾ ounces) condensed cream of chicken soup, undiluted
1 box (6 ounces) corn bread stuffing mix
1 cup chopped onion
1 cup diced red bell pepper
1 cup chopped celery
1 cup frozen corn
3 eggs, lightly beaten

slow cooker directions

1. Lightly coat inside of slow cooker with nonstick cooking spray.

2. Cook chorizo in large skillet over medium-high heat until browned, stirring to break up meat. Transfer to slow cooker.

3. Whisk broth and soup into drippings in skillet over low heat. Add stuffing mix, onion, pepper, celery, corn and eggs; stir until well blended. Stir into slow cooker. Cover; cook on LOW 7 hours or on HIGH 3½ hours.

prep time: 15 minutes • **cook time:** 7 hours (LOW) or 3½ hours (HIGH)

greek rice
makes 6 to 8 servings

2 tablespoons butter
1¾ cups uncooked converted long grain rice
2 cans (14 ounces each) reduced-sodium chicken broth
1 teaspoon Greek seasoning
1 teaspoon ground oregano
1 cup pitted kalamata olives, drained and chopped
¾ cup chopped roasted red peppers
Crumbled feta cheese (optional)
Chopped fresh Italian parsley (optional)

slow cooker directions

1. Melt butter in large nonstick skillet over medium heat. Add rice; cook and stir 4 minutes or until golden brown. Transfer to slow cooker.

2. Stir in broth, seasoning and oregano. Cover; cook on LOW 4 hours or until liquid is absorbed and rice is tender.

3. Stir in olives and roasted red peppers; cook, uncovered, 5 minutes or until heated through.

4. Garnish with feta cheese and parsley.

scalloped potatoes

makes 6 servings

Vegetable cooking spray

3 pounds Yukon Gold or Eastern potatoes, thinly sliced (about 9 cups)

1 large onion, thinly sliced (about 1 cup)

1 can (10¾ ounces) CAMPBELL'S® Condensed Cream of Mushroom Soup (Regular or 98% Fat Free)

½ cup CAMPBELL'S® Condensed Chicken Broth

1 cup shredded Cheddar or crumbled blue cheese (about 4 ounces)

slow cooker directions

1. Spray the inside of a 6-quart slow cooker with the cooking spray. Layer a third of the potatoes and half of the onion in the cooker. Repeat the layers. Top with the remaining potatoes.

2. Stir the soup and broth in a small bowl. Pour over the potatoes. Cover and cook on HIGH for 4 to 5 hours or until the potatoes are tender.

3. Top the potatoes with the cheese. Cover and let stand for 5 minutes or until the cheese is melted.

prep time: 15 minutes • **cook time:** 4 to 5 hours

barley with currants and pine nuts

makes 4 servings

1 tablespoon butter
1 onion, finely chopped
2 cups chicken or vegetable broth
½ cup uncooked pearl barley
½ teaspoon salt
¼ teaspoon black pepper
⅓ cup currants
¼ cup pine nuts

slow cooker directions

1. Melt butter in small skillet over medium-high heat. Add onion; cook 5 minutes or until lightly browned, stirring occasionally. Transfer to slow cooker.

2. Add broth, barley, salt and pepper. Stir in currants. Cover; cook on LOW 3 hours.

3. Stir in pine nuts; serve immediately.

prep time: 10 minutes • **cook time:** 3 hours

tip: Pine nuts are actually seeds that grow inside the cones of several varieties of pine trees. Purchase pine nuts in health food stores, nut shops or larger supermarkets. Store pine nuts in a plastic bag or airtight container and refrigerate up to 3 months or freeze up to 9 months.

simmered red beans with rice

makes 4 to 6 servings

2 cans (about 15 ounces each) red beans, rinsed and drained
1 can (about 14 ounces) diced tomatoes
½ **cup chopped celery**
½ **cup chopped green bell pepper**
½ **cup chopped green onions**
2 cloves garlic, minced
1 to 2 teaspoons hot pepper sauce
1 teaspoon Worcestershire sauce
1 bay leaf
Hot cooked rice

slow cooker directions

1. Combine beans, tomatoes, celery, bell pepper, green onions, garlic, hot pepper sauce, Worcestershire sauce and bay leaf in slow cooker.

2. Cover; cook on LOW 4 to 6 hours or on HIGH 2 to 3 hours.

3. Slightly mash mixture in slow cooker with potato masher to thicken. Cover; cook on LOW 30 to 60 minutes.

4. Remove and discard bay leaf before serving. Serve over rice.

tip: Red beans and rice is a classic example of Louisiana home cooking. Typically, the dish includes chopped ham or bacon, adding a meaty richness to an already hearty dish. This addition has been omitted here to create a dish that is more suited to being a supporting player in a larger meal.

braised sweet and sour cabbage and apples

makes 4 to 6 servings

   2 tablespoons unsalted butter
   6 cups coarsely shredded red cabbage
   1 apple, peeled and cut into bite-size
       pieces
   ½ cup raisins
   ½ cup apple cider
   3 tablespoons cider vinegar, divided
   2 tablespoons packed dark brown sugar
   ½ teaspoon salt
   ¼ teaspoon black pepper
   3 whole cloves

slow cooker directions

1. Melt butter in 12-inch skillet over medium heat. Add cabbage; cook and stir 3 minutes or until glossy. Transfer to slow cooker.

2. Add apple, raisins, apple cider, 2 tablespoons vinegar, brown sugar, salt, pepper and cloves. Cover; cook on LOW 2½ to 3 hours.

3. To serve, remove and discard cloves. Stir in remaining 1 tablespoon vinegar.

prep time: 15 minutes • **cook time:** 2½ to 3 hours

slow cooker spanish rice

makes 6 servings

1 pound BOB EVANS® Original Recipe Sausage Roll
1 can (28 ounces) diced tomatoes
2 cups water
1 small green pepper, diced
2 tablespoons Worchestershire sauce
1 tablespoon chili powder
1 cup long grain rice

slow cooker directions

In medium skillet over medium heat, crumble and cook sausage until brown. Place in slow cooker.

Add tomatoes, water, green pepper, Worchestershire sauce, chili powder and rice. Stir gently to combine.

Cover; cook on LOW for 6 to 8 hours.

substitution: To use instant rice rather than long grain rice, you'll need to add 2 cups instant rice, but do not add it at the beginning. Stir in the instant rice during the last 20 minutes of cooking.

prep time: 10 minutes • **cook time:** 6 to 8 hours

polenta-style corn casserole

makes 6 servings

1 can (about 14 ounces) vegetable broth
½ cup cornmeal
1 can (7 ounces) corn, drained
1 can (4 ounces) diced green chiles, drained
¼ cup diced red bell pepper
½ teaspoon salt
¼ teaspoon black pepper
1 cup (4 ounces) shredded Cheddar cheese

slow cooker directions

1. Pour broth into slow cooker. Whisk in cornmeal. Stir in corn, chiles, bell pepper, salt and black pepper.

2. Cover; cook on LOW 4 to 5 hours or on HIGH 2 to 3 hours.

3. Stir in Cheddar cheese. Cook, uncovered, 15 to 30 minutes or until cheese is melted.

serving suggestion: Divide cooked corn mixture into lightly greased individual ramekins or spread in pie plate; cover and refrigerate. Serve at room temperature or warm in oven or microwave.

blue cheese potatoes
makes 5 servings

2 pounds new red potatoes, peeled and cut into ½-inch pieces
1¼ cups chopped green onions, divided
2 tablespoons olive oil, divided
1 teaspoon dried basil
½ teaspoon salt
¼ teaspoon black pepper
2 ounces crumbled blue cheese

slow cooker directions

1. Layer potatoes, 1 cup green onions, 1 tablespoon oil, basil, salt and pepper in slow cooker.

2. Cover; cook on LOW 7 hours or on HIGH 4 hours.

3. Gently stir in blue cheese and remaining 1 tablespoon oil. Transfer potatoes to serving platter and top with remaining ¼ cup green onions.

tip: The variety of blue cheese you choose to use in this recipe will greatly affect the flavor of the finished dish. Typically, prepackaged cheeses found in large supermarkets will be milder and more agreeable to a broad range of palates than the exotic and pungent strains found in specialty cheese shops. If you are a blue cheese novice, the pre-crumbled variety found in many supermarket cheese cases is a great place to start experimenting with this unique culinary treat.

cheesy broccoli casserole
makes 4 to 6 servings

  2 packages (10 ounces each) frozen chopped broccoli, thawed
  1 can (10¾ ounces) condensed cream of potato soup, undiluted
  1¼ cups (5 ounces) shredded sharp Cheddar cheese, divided
  ¼ cup minced onion
  1 teaspoon hot pepper sauce
  1 cup crushed potato chips or saltine crackers

slow cooker directions

1. Lightly grease slow cooker. Combine broccoli, soup, 1 cup Cheddar cheese, onion and hot pepper sauce in slow cooker; mix well.

2. Cover; cook on LOW 5 to 6 hours or on HIGH 2½ to 3 hours.

3. Sprinkle chips and remaining ¼ cup cheese over broccoli mixture. Cook, uncovered, on LOW 30 to 60 minutes or until cheese is melted.

variation: For a crispy topping, transfer casserole to a baking dish after step 2. Sprinkle with chips and remaining cheese. Bake 10 to 15 minutes in preheated 400°F oven.

slow cooker spinach risotto

makes 4 servings

   2 teaspoons butter
   2 teaspoons olive oil
   3 tablespoons finely chopped shallots
1¼ cups uncooked arborio rice
   ½ cup dry white wine
   3 cups chicken broth
   2 cups baby spinach
   ¼ cup grated Parmesan cheese
   2 tablespoons pine nuts, toasted

slow cooker directions

1. Heat butter and oil in medium skillet over medium heat until butter is melted. Add shallots; cook and stir 1 minute or until softened.

2. Stir in rice; cook 2 minutes or until well coated. Stir in wine and cook until reduced by half. Transfer to slow cooker. Stir in broth.

3. Cover; cook on HIGH 2 to 2½ hours or until rice is almost tender.

4. Stir in spinach. Cover; cook 15 to 20 minutes or until spinach is wilted and rice is tender and creamy.

5. Stir in Parmesan cheese and pine nuts just before serving.

cheese grits with chiles and bacon

makes 4 servings

6 strips bacon, divided
1 serrano or jalapeño pepper,* minced
1 large shallot or small onion, finely chopped
4 cups chicken broth
1 cup uncooked grits**
¼ teaspoon black pepper
Salt
1 cup (4 ounces) shredded Cheddar cheese
½ cup half-and-half
2 tablespoons finely chopped green onion

*Hot peppers can sting and irritate the skin, so wear rubber gloves when handling peppers and do not touch your eyes.

**You may use coarse, instant, yellow or stone-ground grits.

slow cooker directions

1. Cook bacon in medium skillet over medium heat until crisp. Remove bacon and drain on paper towels. Crumble 2 strips and place in slow cooker. Crumble and refrigerate remaining bacon.

2. Drain all but 1 tablespoon bacon drippings from skillet. Add serrano pepper and shallot; cook and stir 2 minutes or until shallot is lightly browned. Transfer to slow cooker.

3. Stir broth, grits, black pepper and salt into slow cooker. Cover; cook on LOW 4 hours.

4. Stir in cheese and half-and-half. Sprinkle with green onion and reserved bacon.

prep time: 15 minutes • **cook time:** 4 hours

slow-roasted potatoes
makes 3 to 4 servings

16 small new red potatoes
3 tablespoons butter, cubed
1 teaspoon paprika
½ teaspoon salt
¼ teaspoon garlic powder
   Black pepper

slow cooker directions

1. Combine potatoes, butter, paprika, salt and garlic powder in slow cooker; mix well. Season with pepper.

2. Cover; cook on LOW 7 hours or on HIGH 4 hours.

3. Transfer potatoes to serving dish with slotted spoon; cover to keep warm.

4. Add 1 to 2 tablespoons water to slow cooker and stir until well blended. Pour mixture over potatoes.

tip: The phrase "new potatoes" refers specifically to young potatoes that have not spent any time in storage. They are typically available in the spring and early summer when crops have been established but the potatoes have not yet reached their full size. If new potatoes are not available because of seasonality, you may substitute small red potatoes with good results.

new england baked beans
makes 4 to 6 servings

    4 slices bacon, chopped
    3 cans (about 15 ounces each) Great
        Northern beans, rinsed and drained
 ³⁄₄ cup water
    1 onion, chopped
 ¹⁄₃ cup canned diced tomatoes, well drained
    3 tablespoons packed light brown sugar
    3 tablespoons maple syrup
    3 tablespoons molasses
    2 cloves garlic, minced
 ¹⁄₂ teaspoon salt
 ¹⁄₂ teaspoon ground mustard
 ¹⁄₈ teaspoon black pepper
    1 bay leaf

slow cooker directions

1. Cook bacon in large skillet over medium heat until chewy but not crisp. Drain on paper towels.

2. Combine bacon, beans, water, onion, tomatoes, brown sugar, maple syrup, molasses, garlic, salt, mustard, pepper and bay leaf in slow cooker; mix well.

3. Cover; cook on LOW 6 to 8 hours. Remove and discard bay leaf before serving.

orange-spiced sweet potatoes

makes 6 to 8 servings

2 pounds sweet potatoes, peeled and diced
½ cup packed dark brown sugar
½ cup butter (1 stick), cubed
Juice of 1 medium orange
1 teaspoon ground cinnamon
1 teaspoon vanilla
½ teaspoon ground nutmeg
½ teaspoon grated orange peel
¼ teaspoon salt
Chopped toasted pecans (optional)

slow cooker directions

1. Combine sweet potatoes, brown sugar, butter, orange juice, cinnamon, vanilla, nutmeg, orange peel and salt in slow cooker.

2. Cover; cook on LOW 4 hours or on HIGH 2 hours.

3. Sprinkle with pecans just before serving, if desired.

variation: Mash sweet potatoes with a hand masher or electric mixer; add ¼ cup milk or whipping cream for a moister consistency. Sprinkle with a mixture of sugar and ground cinnamon.

cheesy corn and peppers
makes 8 servings

2 pounds frozen corn
2 poblano peppers, seeded and chopped
2 tablespoons butter, cubed
1 teaspoon salt
½ teaspoon ground cumin
¼ teaspoon black pepper
1 cup (4 ounces) sharp Cheddar cheese
1 package (3 ounces) cream cheese, cubed

slow cooker directions

1. Coat slow cooker with nonstick cooking spray. Add corn, poblano peppers, butter, salt, cumin and black pepper.

2. Cover; cook on HIGH 2 hours or until corn and poblano peppers are tender.

3. Add Cheddar cheese and cream cheese; stir to blend. Cover; cook 15 minutes or until cheeses are melted.

prep time: 5 minutes • **cook time:** 2¼ hours

cuban black beans and rice

makes 4 to 6 servings

3¾ cups vegetable broth
1½ cups uncooked brown rice
1 onion, chopped
1 jalapeño pepper,* seeded and chopped
3 cloves garlic, minced
2 teaspoons ground cumin
1 teaspoon salt
2 cans (about 15 ounces each) black beans, rinsed and drained
1 tablespoon lime juice
   Sour cream (optional)
   Chopped green onions (optional)

*Jalapeño peppers can sting and irritate the skin, so wear rubber gloves when handling peppers and do not touch your eyes.

slow cooker directions

1. Combine broth, rice, onion, jalapeño pepper, garlic, cumin and salt in slow cooker; mix well.

2. Cover; cook on LOW 7½ hours.

3. Stir in beans and lime juice. Cover; cook 15 to 20 minutes or until beans are heated through.

4. Garnish with sour cream and green onions.

five-bean casserole
makes 16 servings

   2 onions, chopped
   8 ounces bacon, diced
   2 cloves garlic, minced
   ½ cup packed brown sugar
   ½ cup cider vinegar
   1 teaspoon salt
   1 teaspoon ground mustard
   ¼ teaspoon black pepper
   2 cans (about 15 ounces each) kidney beans, rinsed and drained
   1 can (about 15 ounces) chickpeas, rinsed and drained
   1 can (about 15 ounces) butter beans, rinsed and drained
   1 can (about 15 ounces) Great Northern or cannellini beans,
      rinsed and drained
   1 can (about 15 ounces) baked beans
      Chopped green onions (optional)

slow cooker directions

1. Cook and stir onions, bacon and garlic in large skillet over medium heat until onions are tender; drain. Stir in brown sugar, vinegar, salt, mustard and pepper. Reduce heat to low; simmer 15 minutes.

2. Combine kidney beans, chickpeas, butter beans, Great Northern beans and baked beans in slow cooker. Spoon onion mixture evenly over top.

3. Cover; cook on LOW 6 to 8 hours or on HIGH 3 to 4 hours.

4. Sprinkle with green onions just before serving, if desired.

slow cooker cheddar polenta
makes 8 servings

- **7 cups hot water**
- **2 cups polenta (not "quick-cooking") or coarse-ground yellow cornmeal**
- **2 tablespoons extra virgin olive oil**
- **2 teaspoons salt**
- **3 cups grated CABOT® Extra Sharp or Sharp Cheddar (about 12 ounces)**

slow cooker directions

1. Combine water, polenta, olive oil and salt in slow cooker; whisk until well blended. Add cheese and whisk again.

2. Cover; cook on HIGH 2 hours or until most of liquid is absorbed. Stir well. (Polenta should have consistency of thick cooked cereal.)

tip: If you are not planning to serve this delicious polenta right away, pour the mixture onto an oiled baking sheet with sides, spreading into an even layer. Cover with heatproof plastic wrap and let cool. When you are ready to serve, cut the polenta into rectangles and cook in olive oil in a nonstick skillet until golden brown on both sides.

ziti ratatouille
makes 6 servings

**1 large eggplant, peeled and cut into
      ½-inch cubes (about 1½ pounds)**
2 zucchini, cut into ½-inch cubes
**1 green or red bell pepper, cut into ½-inch
      pieces**
1 onion, chopped
4 cloves garlic, minced
1 jar (about 24 ounces) marinara sauce
**2 cans (about 14 ounces each) diced tomatoes with
      garlic and onions**
8 ounces uncooked ziti pasta
1 can (6 ounces) pitted black olives, drained
      Lemon juice (optional)
      Shaved Parmesan cheese (optional)

slow cooker directions
1. Layer eggplant, zucchini, bell pepper, onion, garlic, marinara sauce and tomatoes in slow cooker.

2. Cover and cook on LOW 4½ hours.

3. Stir in pasta and olives. Cover; cook 25 minutes.

4. Drizzle with lemon juice and sprinkle with Parmesan cheese just before serving, if desired.

scalloped tomatoes and corn

makes 4 to 6 servings

   1 can (15 ounces) cream-style corn
   1 can (about 14 ounces) diced tomatoes
 ¾ cup saltine cracker crumbs
   1 egg, lightly beaten
   2 teaspoons sugar
 ¾ teaspoon black pepper
     Chopped fresh tomatoes (optional)
     Chopped fresh Italian parsley (optional)

slow cooker directions

1. Combine corn, diced tomatoes, cracker crumbs, egg, sugar and pepper in slow cooker; mix well.

2. Cover; cook on LOW 4 to 6 hours.

3. Sprinkle with tomatoes and parsley just before serving, if desired.

prep time: 5 minutes • **cook time:** 4 to 6 hours

chunky ranch potatoes
makes 8 servings

3 pounds unpeeled new red potatoes, quartered
1 cup water
½ cup ranch dressing
½ cup grated Parmesan or Cheddar cheese
¼ cup minced chives

slow cooker directions

1. Place potatoes and water in slow cooker.

2. Cover; cook on LOW 8 hours or on HIGH 4 hours.

3. Stir in ranch dressing, Parmesan cheese and chives. Break up potatoes into chunks.

prep time: 10 minutes • **cook time:** 8 hours (LOW) or 4 hours (HIGH)

tip: Everybody loves the creamy tang of ranch dressing and these potatoes couldn't be easier to make. You don't even have to peel them. The ruby skins of these red potatoes add much needed color to the dish, while saving you time on preparation, helping the potatoes keep their shape during the extended cooking time, and ensuring that all the nutritious fiber found in the skins makes it onto the plate.

index

acknowledgments

The publisher would like to thank the companies and organizations listed below for the use of their recipes and photographs in this publication.

Bob Evans®

Cabot® Creamery Cooperative

Campbell Soup Company

Reckitt Benckiser Inc.

metric conversion chart

VOLUME MEASUREMENTS (dry)

⅛ teaspoon = 0.5 mL
¼ teaspoon = 1 mL
½ teaspoon = 2 mL
¾ teaspoon = 4 mL
1 teaspoon = 5 mL
1 tablespoon = 15 mL
2 tablespoons = 30 mL
¼ cup = 60 mL
⅓ cup = 75 mL
½ cup = 125 mL
⅔ cup = 150 mL
¾ cup = 175 mL
1 cup = 250 mL
2 cups = 1 pint = 500 mL
3 cups = 750 mL
4 cups = 1 quart = 1 L

VOLUME MEASUREMENTS (fluid)

1 fluid ounce (2 tablespoons) = 30 mL
4 fluid ounces (½ cup) = 125 mL
8 fluid ounces (1 cup) = 250 mL
12 fluid ounces (1½ cups) = 375 mL
16 fluid ounces (2 cups) = 500 mL

WEIGHTS (mass)

½ ounce = 15 g
1 ounce = 30 g
3 ounces = 90 g
4 ounces = 120 g
8 ounces = 225 g
10 ounces = 285 g
12 ounces = 360 g
16 ounces = 1 pound = 450 g

DIMENSIONS

1/16 inch = 2 mm
⅛ inch = 3 mm
¼ inch = 6 mm
½ inch = 1.5 cm
¾ inch = 2 cm
1 inch = 2.5 cm

OVEN TEMPERATURES

250°F = 120°C
275°F = 140°C
300°F = 150°C
325°F = 160°C
350°F = 180°C
375°F = 190°C
400°F = 200°C
425°F = 220°C
450°F = 230°C

BAKING PAN SIZES

Utensil	Size in Inches/Quarts	Metric Volume	Size in Centimeters
Baking or Cake Pan (square or rectangular)	8×8×2	2 L	20×20×5
	9×9×2	2.5 L	23×23×5
	12×8×2	3 L	30×20×5
	13×9×2	3.5 L	33×23×5
Loaf Pan	8×4×3	1.5 L	20×10×7
	9×5×3	2 L	23×13×7
Round Layer Cake Pan	8×1½	1.2 L	20×4
	9×1½	1.5 L	23×4
Pie Plate	8×1¼	750 mL	20×3
	9×1¼	1 L	23×3
Baking Dish or Casserole	1 quart	1 L	—
	1½ quart	1.5 L	—
	2 quart	2 L	—